AF539825

SCHOOL SUBJECTS
ISSUES AND CONCERNS

SCHOOL SUBJECTS
ISSUES AND CONCERNS

By

Prof. Marlow Ediger
B.S.E., M.A., Ed.D. (Education)
Emeritus Professor of Education
Truman State University
201 West 22nd Street
North Newton KS 67117
United States of America
mediger2@cox.net

&

Prof. Digumarti Bhaskara Rao
M.Sc., M.A., M.A., M.Ed., Ph.D.
Chairman
Board of Studies in Education
Acharya Nagarjuna University
Nagarjuna Nagar - 522 510 (India)
&
Principal
R.V.R. College of Education
D-43 (277) S.V.N. Colony
Guntur - 522 006 (India)
digumartibhaskararao@rediffmail.com

DISCOVERY PUBLISHING HOUSE PVT. LTD.
NEW DELHI-110 002

Published by:

Tilak Wasan

DISCOVERY PUBLISHING HOUSE PVT. LTD.

4383/4B, Ansari Road, Darya Ganj
New Delhi-110 002 (India)
Phone : +91-11-23279245, 43596064-65
Fax : +91-11-23253475
E-mail : discoverypublishinghouse@gmail.com
sales@discoverypublishinggroup.com
parul.wasan@gmail.com
web : www.discoverypublishinggroup.com

***First Edition:* 2014**

ISBN: 978-93-5056-433-2

School Subjects: *Issues and Concerns*

Printed at:
Dynamic Printers
Delhi

Dedicated
to

Mrs. Mary Duerksen Ediger

Books by **Marlow Ediger**
& Digumarti Bhaskara Rao

Administration of Schools
Community Colleges
Curriculum Organisation
Curriculum of School Subjects
Curriculum, School and Teacher
Effective Schooling
Effective School Curriculum
Elementary Curriculum
Elementary Curriculum Improvement
Essays on School Curriculum
Essays on School Issues
Essays on Teaching Mathematics
Essays on Teaching Science
Essays on Teaching Social Studies
Essays on Teaching Reading
Essays on Teaching and Learning
Improving School Administration
Issues in School Curriculum
Language Arts Curriculum
Philosophy and Curriculum
Psychology and Curriculum
Quality School Education
Reading Curriculum and Instruction
Relevancy in Elementary Curriculum
School Organisation
School Curriculum and Administration
School Curriculum and Teaching
Science Curriculum
Teaching English Successfully
Teaching Language Arts Successfully
Teaching Mathematics Successfully
Teaching Science Successfully
Teaching Social Studies Successfully
Teaching Mathematics in Elementary Schools
Teaching Science in Elementary Schools
Successful School Administration
Successful School Education

Preface

School is an institution designed for the teaching of students under the direction of teachers. The primary school is meant for young children and the secondary school is for teenagers who have completed their primary schooling.

School is a place where students are moulded to the requirements of personal as well as public life through curriculum transaction. The curriculum comprising of different subjects need special attention from teachers and administrators as their implementation involves several issues and concerns.

Many issues and concerns concerned to school subjects are discussed in detail in this book. This book will be of great use to the curriculum specialists, textbook writers, teachers and administrators at school stages.

Sri Sai Soudha
D-43 S.V.N.
Guntur-522006
India

Marlow Ediger
Digumarti Bhaskarao Rao

Contents

The Integrated Science Curriculum

Pupils need to perceive that subject matter is related in different curriculum areas. It becomes easier to retain learnings if content is sensed as being related. One idea then makes it less complex to relate to others. The degree to which content should be related becomes an issue. How much of subject matter integration should then be emphasized in teaching and learning situations? This might be shown on a continuum, all the way from very minimal to much integration of subject matter taught. A strong consideration here pertains to which science unit of study is being emphasized and how much of meaningful relationships can be shown with other academic disciplines.

Science and the Integration of Subject Matter

Science has its own unique facts, concepts and generalizations which pupils need to acquire from the earth sciences, the physical sciences, and the biological sciences. Relevant objectives then need to be determined which learners need to attain. The objectives need to be challenging and attainable. Objectives which are too difficult to achieve make for feelings of frustration whereas those being too easy might well make for boredom. Then too, there needs to be a balance among knowledge, skills, and attitudinal ends. Learner achievement needs to be evaluated during the time a unit is taught as well as at the end of the unit. A variety of appraisal techniques must be used in the evaluation process such as:

- teacher daily observation and appraised in terms of quality criteria.
- pupil self-evaluation, reflection and metacognition.
- valid and reliable multiple choice and essay test items, teacher developed or mandated tests.
- assessment of science projects developed.
- evaluation of critical and creative thinking as well as problem solving skills.
- appraisal of listening, speaking, reading and writing skills in science (See National Science Education Standards, 1996).

With integration of subject matter, the science teacher needs to decide at which point this should occur. The integration must be seamless and add value to what is being studied. Thus, integration is not done for the sake of doing so, but rather to project meaning in achieving relevant objectives. The integrated science curriculum has numerous advan-tages:

- it assists pupils to extend knowledge beyond the study of a single academic discipline. However, a pupil should always gain adequate knowledge of what science is and its methods used, to acquire information.
- it helps pupils to related science to other academic disciplines. The transfer of knowledge and its use from discipline to discipline might guide pupils to achieve more optimally. Pupils should, however, perceive the content and processes of science pertaining to one academic discipline.
- it promotes pupil learning across the curriculum such as in reading subject matter. Science concepts and generalizations and their meanings are unique to one academic discipline as are those of each of the other academic disciplines.
- it has specific kinds of learning activities such as doing experiments which is the heart of the science curri-

culum; others cut across several academic disciplines such as inquiry learning, problem solving, project methods, critical and creative thinking, as well as cooperative learning.

- it stresses evaluation in terms of teacher observation to notice achievement such as in experimentation, as a learning activity, which requires clarity of criteria to assess the quality of problem identified, the hypotheses developed and the testing of each tentative hypothesis (Ediger and Rao, 2007).

Separate Subjects Discipline and Committee Endeavors

When supervising university student teachers in the public schools, the writer observed the teaching of a sixth grade science unit on invertebrates. The student teacher and the cooperating teacher adhered to teaching specific facts, concepts and generalizations pertaining to science as a separate academic discipline. Very little attention was given to integrating subject matter from other academic disciplines. Pupils then divided into committees to work on a report of their chosen topic from a list developed by the student teacher and the cooperating teacher. Each committee could then select which classification of invertebrates they wished to work from in gathering necessary information.

The following were listed and both teachers stressed background information on each during the large group sessions:

- the ameba, the paramecium and the euglena (protozoans)
- sponges (porifera)
- hydras, jellyfish, coral and sea anemones (coelenterates)
- flatworms such as planarians, flukes and tapeworms (platyhelminthes)
- segmented worms like earthworms and sandworms (annelida)
- starfish, sea urchin, sea cucumber and sand dollar (echinodermata)

- clams, scallops, mussels, oysters, slugs and snails (mollusca)
- shrimp, lobster, crayfish and crabs (arthropods) (See Blough and Schwartz, 1984).

Criteria for working on each committee were discussed and standards for presenting the oral reports were also given. A variety of reference sources were used to gather needed information. One committee chose "shrimp and lobster" for their oral reports. The details of each were developed indepth. In addition to reporting on these two invertebrates, knowledge from other disciplines were integrated into the oral report such as:

- seafood served in restaurants which include shrimp and lobster.
- large scale fishing for shrimp and lobster, as a means of earning a living.
- raising these invertebrates in farm operations.
- characteristics making for the classification of "arthropods".

A second committee chose "earthworms" for their investigation. They described the classification of invertebrates such as "annelids" indepth. In addition to the scientific classification, the committee also integrated the following from other academic subject matter areas:

- earthworms being a part of compost piles.
- their role in maintaining fertile soils.
- earthworms eaten as food in certain nations.
- characteristics of invertebrates known as "annelida".

For example, in each of the social science disciplines, invertebrates may be studied from their separate subject area:

- economics as in ways of earning a livelihood such as fishing for oysters.
- regions in geography where specific invertebrates are located.

- history in the study of rare species and those no longer in existence.
- sociology and the indepth knowledge of culture involving exotic foods such as chocolate covered, fried grasshoppers.
- political science with its rules and regulations on fishing for shrimp and lobster.

There are selected criteria which need to be followed in developing an integrated science curriculum. Science content must be at the center of the planning. The principles of science must not be overshadowed by content from other academic disciplines. The latter must enhance the planned science unit of study. Objectives for pupil attainment need to be carefully chosen in terms of being relevant and useful in school and in society. They must be ordered or sequenced to optimize learner achievement and progress. Learning activities should be aligned with the stated objectives. They need to be interesting, meaningful and possess purpose. Appraisal procedures need to be varied to take into account the assessment of experimentation. It is difficult for paper/pencil tests to measure achievement adequately in this salient facet of learning. Teacher observation in terms of important criteria must be used here. Otherwise, multiple choice and essay tests may be used to measure acquired facts, concepts, and generalizations in science. Tests must be valid and reliable (See National Research Council, 2000).

Pertaining to the integration and relationship of different academic disciplines, Jackson *et al.*, 2008) wrote the following:

> Making connections is always an important task for teachers. Science teachers are encouraged to connect new learnings with student's prior knowledge, learning with student interests, learning with cultural experiences and classroom activities across academic disciplines. Strategies that facilitate these connections help teachers enrich and enhance instruction.

REFERENCES

Blough, Glenn and Schwartz, Julius (1984), *Elementary School Science and How to Teach It.* New York: CBS Publishing Company.

Ediger, Marlow and Digumarti Bhaskara Rao (2007), *School Science Education*. New Delhi, India: Discovery Publishing House (Ltd.).

Jackson, Julie, *et al.*, (2008), "Connections, Charts and Book Talks," *Science and Children*, 46 (3), 27-31.

National Research Council (2000), *How People Learn*. Washington, DC: National Academy Press.

National Science Education Standards (1996), National Research Council. Washington, DC: The Academy Press.

Leadership to Improve the Science Curriculum

The science curriculum needs to be studied and updated periodically. The best objectives, learning activities and appraisal procedures need to be implemented. Each of us lives in a scientific world. The knowledge explosion in science has been here for some time. New medical practices to improve and prolong life, better means of producing goods and services, as well as innovative means of transportation and communication, among others, have helped to make for a more meaningful and quality life style.

There also are hindrances to an improved society such as wars which and maim military personnel as well as civilians, destroy buildings, pollute and make for hatred toward others. These, among other problems, need identification and solutions made.

To have appropriate and needed innovations in the science curriculum, leadership is necessary. Within a public school setting, there are individuals and groups which may provide the needed leadership. One person may be designated to carry on the role of being a leader to improve the science curriculum, namely the school principal. However, each teacher might also be a leader in working toward a quality science curriculum (Edigei and Rao 2007).

Efforts Toward Improving the Science Curriculum

Grade level meetings are one method to use in science curriculum improvement. Thus, within the building, fourth grade teachers, as an example, may meet together in a planned series of meetings. If the school has only two teachers per grade level, combining fourth, fifth and sixth grade science teachers is a good possibility. As one task of the group, objectives may be discussed and be more specific as compared those on mandated tests. Meaningful, agreed upon objectives for student achievement is important. Vague, hazy objectives may not be of much assistance to the science teacher. By discussing objectives, the involved teachers may also notice omitted relevant objectives such as critical and creative thinking, as well as problem solving. Attitudinal objectives, also, may be slighted unless emphasized in teaching (Ediger, 2008).

Along with discussing objectives, these science teachers may also assess the learning activities to achieve each objective. Here, teachers learn about different possibilities to assist learners to achieve, grow and develop. Too frequently, teachers have used the same kinds of activities which have not motivated students. Perhaps, too much stress has been placed upon reading about science rather than doing science experiments and demonstrations. There needs to be rational balance among diverse kinds of learning experiences such as concrete, semi-concrete and abstract activities (Ediger, 2007-2008). In addition to experimentation and reading, the following also need to be considered as possibilities to provide for individual differences:

- whole class and peer discussion groups.
- construction activities such as making a solar collector in an ongoing unit of study.
- art work such as developing a science mural illustrating a concept and/or generalization.
- poetry writing directly related to an ongoing lesson.
- reading and reporting on a library book involving a specific topic in science.
- debates such as advocating a specific for of energy such as wind, water, solar, nuclear, coal, geothermal, among others.

- dramatic activities including the life of a famous scientist.
- individualized reading on a self chosen science library book (See Hansen, 2003).

The teachers in the inservice education experience need to view valid and reliable evaluation techniques to appraise progress which may well include:

- student and teacher self-evaluation in terms of desired criteria.
- teacher observation, using recommended standards, to assess and diagnose/remediate.
- teacher written tests such as essay and multiple choice test items.

Grade level meetings should aid to improve the science curriculum. Teacher feedback to the group of what seemingly was successful in the classroom from the involved discussions needs to be analyzed and reported upon (Ediger, 2008).

Faculty meetings may also be devoted to improving science teaching. Problems in teaching science need to be discussed. Ideas presented must be respected and flow freely among participants. Ideas for discussion involving improving the science curriculum may come from any faculty member. An agenda committee should prioritize the problems identified for discussion, if many suggestions are made. The best ideas for teaching science should result from the faculty meeting. A faculty member may volunteer to try out an innovative idea in the classroom and report back to the group. Then too, committees may be formed in volunteering to work on a problem area. Among others, these may include the following:

- using inductive teaching.
- having students engage in problem solving which includes having a tentative solution to the problem in hypothesis form, and then testing the hypothesis.
- developing an integrated science/social studies unit on alternative sources of energy.
- stressing quality sequence in science.

- using writing activities in ongoing lessons and units of study (See Ohanian and Kovacs, 2007).

An additional approach at inservice education is the workshop concept. Faculty members need to be surveyed to ascertain which facets of science instruction need the most emphasis. Items in the survey need to be clearly stated with participants indicating their first, second and third choices to be covered in the workshop. Space in the survey needs to be alloted to an open ended question, "What would you like to see in a quality science workshop?" This gives participants a chance to indicate what they personally would want to experience in improving the science curriculum. The following items in the survey, as an example, may be numbered as to importance by each workshop participant:

- computers and technology use in teaching science.
- use of science library books in ongoing lesson/unit discussions.
- a multi-media emphasis in teaching and learning situations.
- engaging learners in ongoing science lessons and units of study.
- student self monitoring of achievement.
- metacognition strategies in teaching and learning situations (See Zahra, 2008).

There needs to be adequate time for participants to appraise the value of the workshop. Feedback is necessary to increase the usefulness of workshops to improve the science curriculum. Science teachers need to feel that inservice education programs are truly effective to provide students with the best objectives, learning opportunities and assessment procedures.

Then too, teachers may take science education courses online or at an approved university. The course work may lead to an advanced degree in graduate studies. The degree program should include course work in educational psychology, science education and science content. School principals need to publicize university offerings which might well meet the needs of science teachers. The local school library should have a section devoted to journals and teacher education textbooks pertaining to science and science education. A convenient setting for teachers to read the science materials needs to be in the offing (See Biddle and Saha, 2006).

The Psychology of Teaching Science

There are selected principles of learning which science teachers need to implement in teaching and learning situations. This must go much beyond the recall level of subject matter presented by the teacher. Thus, students need to analyze content while engaging in lessons and units of study to separate the relevant from the irrelevant as well as the accurate from the inaccurate. This is needed to provide the best information in the solving of problems. Creative thinking, too, is necessary to come up with novel, new ideas. Innovations come about in society due to creative thinking. Novel, unique ideas are then wanted. The worth of an idea needs assessment and involves evaluation (See Cuniff and McMillen, 1996).

Creating and developing interest in an ongoing science lesson/unit of study is salient. With interest, students ask questions and explore possible answers. The curious learner is one who will grow in the ability to acquire knowledge, skills, and attitudes. An open mind is willing to venture out into the unknown and find gaps in knowledge and skills with the intent of attempting to close the gap.

Metacognitive skills must be achieved. Here, the student, with teacher help, engages in thinking about thinking. Thus, for example, the student reflects upon how he/she evaluated the worth of an idea or how a problem was identified for solving. Additional examples of metacognition include reflection upon how the student:

- arrived at an answer or solution to a problem.
- followed a specific sequence in problem solving following a science experiment with the intent of viewing what was missing in the procedure.

- engaged in committee work to make for a successful endeavor.

Meaning is always salient to stress in any learning experience. To understand what was taught is of utmost importance. Otherwise, hazy, vague understandings are not useful in building upon those previous learnings. To extend learnings, meaning must be attached to what has transpired.

Purpose for student learning must also be emphasized. Reasons then are accepted by the student for achieving objectives of instruction. The purpose for each activity in science needs to be clearly stated by the teacher/learner and, hopefully, accepted by the latter (See National Research Council, 1989).

REFERENCES

Biddle, Bruce and Lawrence J. Saha (2006), "How Principals Use Research," *Educational Leadership*, 63 (6), 72-78.

Cuniff, Patricia A. and Janet K. McMillen (1996), "Field Studies," *The Science Teacher*, 63 (5), 55-60.

Ediger, Marlow (2007), *Science Curriculum and Instruction*. New Delhi, India: Discovery Publishing House (Ltd.).

Ediger, Marlow (2008), "Mental Health in the Curriculum," *Edutracks*, 7 (7), 13-1 5. Published in India.

Ediger, Marlow (2008), "Training Staff to Teach Reading in the Content Areas," *Leadership Compass*, 5(3), 1-2. Published by the National Association of Elementary School Principals.

Ediger, Marlow (2007-2008), "Student Vocabulary Development in Science," *Connecticut Journal of Science Education*, 45(1), 12-13.

Hansen, Laurie (2003), "Science in Any Language," *Science and Children*, 41 (3), 35-39.

National Research Council (1989), *National Science Standards*. Washington, DC: National Academy Press.

Ohanian, Susan and Philip Kovacs (2007), "Make Room at the Table for Teachers, 89 (4), 270-274.

Zahra, Anne (2008), "Limitless Images: Digital Photography in the Classroom," *The Delta Kappa Gamma Bulletin*, 75 (1), 7-9,17.

Reading Comprehension in the Science Curriculum

Students may experience difficulty in reading science subject matter. It is very important that each comprehends well when reading content in science as well as understanding these ideas indepth. The teacher needs to help each student in comprehending when being engaged in reading to secure facts, concepts, and generalizations in science (See Cuniff and McMillen 1996). What might be done to assist learners in achieving when reading?

Increasing Reading Comprehension in Science

Reading may be done to secure background information in attaching meaning to a science experiment. Readiness in benefiting from the experiment is a must. Necessary background knowledge for reading then needs to be activated in in order to understand subject matter in the ongoing activity.

Reading may also be done to substantiate, modify, or refute student conclusions realized from the science experiment. It might be necessary to redo the experiment and/or view other reference sources to test the outcomes of the initial science experiment. In supervising university student teachers in the public schools, the writer observed a student teacher and the cooperating teacher viewing and discussing related illustrations from a basal science science textbook. Much interest was developed to pursue the reading experience. New words which appeared in the scripted materials were printed on a flipchart In this way, students could see and take careful notice during the discussion of each as they were used in the textbook. Questions pertaining to the textbook illustrations were identified and printed on the chalkboard. They were referred to in the reading activity. These experiences provided readiness for reading science subject matter and all were related to the science experiment discussed above (Ediger, 2007).

If the students in the class are homogeneously grouped and are good readers, the illustrations, alone, may be discussed to motivate the class in the reading activity. Otherwise, fluency in reading should also occur. Reading hesitantly and haltingly hinders comprehension in reading experiences. Readiness experiences assist in avoiding these situations.

There are a plethora of followup activities in reading and might well include the following:

- check the conclusions with that of the science experiment.
- develop a related science experiment.
- write up the conclusions within a committee and file for future reference.
- do a diorama, write poetry, and/or make a drawing of the completed science experiment.
- in a peer setting, identify a project to complete and/or.
- make a model, related to the experiment.
- put new science words encountered on the science wall.
- develop a bulletin board display (Ediger, 2008).

Strategies to Stress in Teaching

The difficulties in reading to understand science subject matter may be minimized with foresight and skilful methods used in teaching. A university student teacher (ST) supervised by the writer in the public schools used an opaque projector to enlarge the print contained in the basal textbook so all could see the content clearly in a small group of five struggling readers. She discussed the related illustrations to develop background information for the reading activity. The purpose also was stated for reading the science subject matter. The ST read the content aloud while pointing to each word/phrase. Students were carefully observed and assisted to follow the script carefully while the subject matter was read orally. The second reading followed with the teacher and students reading aloud together as the former still pointed to each word being read. Then students in the small group read the content collectively without teacher help. The latter still pointed to each word being read. Students generally were able to read the selection independently. In this way, students developed a basic science vocabulary and comprehended subject matter read. Later, these students participated with the others in discussing vital science concepts and generalizations, such as motion, matter, friction and force. By using this procedure, struggling readers may:

- read the same ideas as others in the classroom.
- read fluently without stumbling on unknown words.
- read science subject matter, concentrating on comprehension.
- read in gaining a basic sight vocabulary through rereading science subject matter in a non-threatening manner (See Gill, 2008).

In all procedures of science reading instruction, students need to monitor, individually, their very own comprehension of subject matter. By monitoring what has been read, students may reflect upon comprehended facts, concepts and generalizations and not merely pronouncing words while reading. Metacognition strategies, also, are important. Here, students are taught to think about thinking. Thus, the student thinks, for example, about the central idea of all the inherent ideas acquired. Parts are then synthesized into a complex whole. Metacognition may also be emphasized in rehearsing what has been learned to notice gaps in knowledge and skills.

Thus, there may be gaps in the past problem or project completed with involved knowledge and skills. Gaps can be ameliorated through a process known as scaffolding. Here, the science teacher notices where a student is in achievement presently and compares it with a developmentally more complex ideal. This gap may be minimized with a set of carefully planned, sequential learning experiences (Ediger and Rao, 2007).

In Conclusion

To show excellence in comprehending science subject matter. Students need assistance to develop background information pertaining to what will be read, thus connecting what is known with what will be read. It is also good to have students relate the content to their very own personal lives in terms of uses to be made of the information. Vocabulary development is an inherent part of becoming a good reader in science. The reading activities need to center around the heart of science which is quality experimentation. Learnings acquired need to be extended to emphasize indepth understanding of vital facts, concepts, and generalizations. Recreational reading, too, needs to be stressed in which accurate science content may be read. The teacher needs to be aware of library books which are available in this area which might interest and challenge learner curiosities (See National Research Council, 1996).

Important trends need to be studied by teachers, including how technology and computers may assist students to achieve complex, but achievable objectives. There needs to be high teacher expectations for each student's achievement! (See Horejsi, 2003).

REFERENCES

Cuniff, Patricia A. and Janet K. McMillen (1996), "Field Studies," *The Science Teacher*, 63, 51-55.

Ediger, Marlow (2007), "Meaning in Reading Instruction," *Reading Improvement*, 44 (4), 217-220.

Ediger, Marlow and D. Bhaskara Rao (2007), *Science Curriculum and Instruction*. New Delhi, India: Discovery Publishing House (Ltd.).

Ediger, Marlow (2008), "Leadership in the School Setting," *Education*, 129(1), 17-20.

Gill, Sharon Ruth (2008), "The Comprehension Matrix: A Tool for Designing Comprehension Strategies," *The Reading Teacher*, 62(2), 106-115.

Horejsi, Martin (2003), "Making Technolgy Inclusive," *Science and Children*, 41 (3), 20-24.

National Researcher Council (1996), *National Science Education Standards*. Washington, DC: the National Academy Press.

The Pupil, Writing and the Science Curriculum

Pupils writing across the curriculum is highly significant. The science curriculum can certainly make its many contributions in having learners become effective writers. Being scientifically literate is essential for all in the age of science. Being able to read and write pertaining to information obtained from science lessons and units of study in the school setting is valuable presently as well as in the future. Ideas must be communicated accurately and with precision. Misinformation occurs due to poor quality means of communicating in the written language. Abstract ideas are communicated which the receiver interprets in the concrete.

A developmentally appropriate science curriculum must be emphasized in teaching and learning situations. Otherwise, science learnings may be either too complex whereby frustration occurs or too simple in which boredom may be an end result. The science teacher must adapt different writing strategies to meet pupil needs (Edigen and Rao, 2007).

Written Communication in Science

Within each lesson and unit of study, the science teacher must plan quality learning experiences which integrate effectively with experiments, demonstrations, multi-media presentations, as well as reading experiences. Written work by pupils needs to be:

- engaging whereby learners are whole-heartedly involved in communicating ideas.

- interesting in terms of experiences provided. Definitely, written work should not "turn" the pupil off in making progress in this area.
- involve communicating ideas as accurately and objectively as possible.
- meaningfully perceived and communicated so the reader/listener can make the abstract message become concrete.
- intrinsically purposeful. Pupils then accept reasons for active participation (See Beckstead, 2008).

Engaging pupils in written work in ongoing science lessons and units of study emphasizes that the teacher provide variety in the kinds of activities provided. Among others, the pupil may write up the steps followed in developing a science fair project for exhibit in the local school district annual contest. In the project, the pupil will need to state the purpose for project. Also included are the plans for its development and how the plans were carried out. Hypotheses to be tested are written clearly. Self evaluation by the pupil should be included such as standards listed pertaining to neatness, completeness, and relevance (See National National Research Council, 1996).

Interesting writing activities should be provided. Different, rich and stimulating experiences must be in the offing. These should include journal writing, diary entries, logs, book reports and summaries. They need to be complete, comprehensive and indepth. Then too, pupils need encouragement to do voluntary writing. A learning center in the classroom needs to list topics directly related to ongoing science lessons. Pupils might then choose tasks to complete, from among others. Quality written work is to be expected. High expectations for a good product is necessary; however learner success at the same time is salient. Failure in achievement makes for a negative self concept. Too many pupils have feelings of being a failure in written work. This image must be changed to assist each pupil to achieve a healthy and wholesome self concept and it is possible to improve sequentially to becoming a better writer (See Barclay and Schoon, 1999).

Writing as accurately as possible requires a rich vocabulary. Vocabulary growth is a definite part of writing proficiency. When writing, the writer wishes to communicate effectively with others. Variety in vocabulary use is necessary to keep the reader's attention. At the same time, it can be very enjoyable to locate synonyms for a given word to provide for variety in written products. The writer when observing university student teachers teach has noticed frequently that word study need not be boring, but does interest many pupils. Sometimes, brain storming has been used to list as many synonyms as possible for a given word. Pupils then provide as many words as possible for a "match" printed word on the chalkboard. They look at dictionaries, thesauruses, among other sources in book or computer form. When ready, the word processor may be used to communicate ideas for book reports, write-ups of science projects and experiments, summaries, log and diary entries, journal writing, among the many other purposes in writing (See Hawkins, 2006).

Since writing is done to communicate with others, it behooves the science teacher to assist pupils to write meaningfully. Sometimes, it is good to have a writer in the classroom share written work with peers to notice the quality of communication involved. Thus, a listener may retell what he/she comprehended from a written product. Did the writer communicate what was intended? Proper punctuation must be used to notice pauses as well as end of sentences. The science teacher may read aloud to pupils eliminating pauses in order for the listener to notice how meanings change with omitted commas, quotation marks, periods, question marks, and exclamation points. Voice inflection in oral reading also must be noticed by pupils when pitching words higher or lower within a sentence. Also, meanings change of a sentence when specific words are stressed more heavily than others within a sentence. Pitch of words is generally not shown in a written product. Sometimes a writer will underline one or more words in a selection to indicate stress of words, meaning they are said louder than the others.

Meaning may also be indicated in writing by putting in main divisions, as well as subdivisions. As a learning experience, these divisions, in bold print, need to be pointed out by the teacher when pupils read from the basal science textbook. They orient the reader to ensuing subject matter to be read (Ediger, 2007).

Reasons for participating in written work must be stressed prior to learner participation in the writing activity. Thus, if pupils are to write for free and inexpensive science materials, the purpose for writing the letter must be clear to the pupil. Then too if this is an initial learning experience, pupils must know the reasons for writing each part of the business letter such as the heading, inside address, body, closing, and signature. Neatness and clarity are salient criteria to use in appraising the quality of the business letter, written either in long hand or with the use of the word process or. When needed, the science teacher may model these and other learnings in the curriculum. Modeling is a powerful tool to use in teaching science.

Strategies to Use in Teaching and Learning

The science teacher needs to model metacognition approaches of learning in ongoing lessons and units of study. Here, the teacher assists pupil to reflect upon what was learned. Thus after completion of a science experiment, pupils might well be guided to reflect upon the following:

- the sequential steps followed in conducting the experiment.
- major concepts and generalizations acquired.
- processes followed in discussing the conducting of and the results of the experiment (Ediger, 2006).

Metacognition strategies emphasize thinking about thinking. Thus, the pupil mentally reviews what was learned, what needs more emphasis in learning, and which questions the pupil would like to do research on or discuss more indepth.

Encouraging thinking is vital in order that the pupil thinks critically and creatively. Optimal achievement in science is a must!

Inductive learning also must receive its fair share of time in science lessons and units of study. To learn inductively, a pupil is not provided with a lecture or lengthy explanation of subject matter content in a lesson, but rather questions are raised to help the learner find needed answers. A high school physics teacher at a National Science Teacher's Association convention stated that he never answered a pupil's questions with facts, but rather asked another question which assisted the pupil in finding necessary information.

In closing

Pupils need a variety of rich experiences in writing. They must experience purpose, interest and meaning in all written work. Writing skills are salient in science but also in the societal arena. The science teacher must integrate written work along with reading, listening and speaking goals in ongoing lessons and units of study.

REFERENCES

Barclay, D. C. and S. Schoon (1999), "Making the Connection! Science and Literacy," *Childhood Education*, 75 (3),1 46-1 52.

Beckstead, Larissa (2008), "Scientific Journals: A Creative Assessment Tool," *Science and Children*, 46 (3), 22-26.

Ediger, Marlow (2006), "Writing in the Mathematics Curriculum," *Journal of Instructional Psychology*, 33 (1), 120-123.

Ediger, Marlow and D. Bhaskara Rao (2007), *Language Arts Education*. New Delhi, India: Discovery Publishing House (Ltd.).

Ediger, Marlow (2007), "Meaning in Reading Instruction", *Reading Improvement*, 44 (4), 21 7-220.

Hawkins, Joanna (2006), "Think Before You Write," *Educational Leadership*, 64 (2), 63-67.

National Research Council (1996), *National Science Education Standards*. Washington, DC: The Academy Press.

5 A Stimulating Science Vocabulary Environment

Student interest in science may be extended through a rich vocabulary environment. Students need to see words and experience them in an interesting way. A variety of approaches need to be emphasized for students to see words in print and relate them to the concrete (objects and items used in teaching science) as well as the semi-concrete (illustrations, pictures, and pictorial representations of reality). Words are abstractions which convey and communicate ideas. A rich speaking, reading, writing and listening vocabulary should assist students to become increasingly science literate (See Zales and Unger, 2008).

Extending Student Learnings in Science

The interests of students need to be piqued in ongoing lessons and units of study in science. A variety of rich experiences must be in the offing which provide for students of diverse achievement levels. One procedure to set up a word wall in the classroom. When interesting new words are identified by students in discussion settings, they need to be printed, large enough for all to see clearly and placed on the word wall. The writer when supervising university student teachers frequently noticed how learners congregate at the word wall, point to, and discuss meanings of these words. The content for discussion may have come from reading subject matter in the basal text. Words tend to fascinate students and encourage interesting comments and use (Ediger and Rao, 2007). How might these words be used?

With readiness involved, several students wrote different types of poetry which included rhymed verse such as couplets, triplets, quatrains and limericks. A few wrote poems containing syllabication such as haiku and tankas. Still others wrote free verse and diamontes. Students had studied each of these kinds of poems previously in the language arts and were enthused in using science words in a creative manner. They also noticed the science/language arts connection.

Pupils being actively involved in sustained silent reading (SSR) was also observed in student teaching by the writer. Here, pupils chose science information and science fiction library books for the self-selected reading activity. Generally, pupils choose library books written on their individual reading level. Pupil were encouraged to do more voluntary reading and in this case science library books. It is difficult to say how much increase in science knowledge accrued in SSR, but the writer feels there is much to gain in subject matter content, skills, and especially attitudes in a voluntary reading activity. Not all achievement is measurable; some must probably be inferred through rational judgement (Ediger and Rao, 2007).

SSR is quite open ended in terms of being sequential learning experiences. Pupils must make many decisions on their very own in terms of which ordered books to read and quality comprehension which is desired from learners. Scaffolded Silent Reading (ScSSR) is more structured with the science teacher assisting in library book selection. When pupils read silently the chosen library book, the teacher randomly asks learners questions covering subject matter read. This is done to evaluate comprehension of science content. A pupil may also be asked to read a short selection aloud to appraise word recognition and fluency in reading.The teacher jots down a few observations made, dated, and with the pupil's name attached (Reutzel, *et al.,* 2008). Progress in securing science facts, concepts and generalizations is then noted for each pupil.

With either SSR or ScSSR, the involved pupil may keep a vocabulary notebook containing what he/she perceives to be important vocabulary terms. In small group sessions or the class as a whole, pupils may share recorded words. Growth in science vocabularies may occur through word walls and summaries of SSR/ScSSR library book reading. Both are available for review and study. It is good to rehearse science words and vocabulary terms to improve retention as well as interest.

Journals need to be kept by pupils of science experiments performed. One part of the write-up for each experiment should be devoted to science terminology used in the activity. Each experiment needs to be clearly visible and meaningful to all in the small group as well as those taught in large group instruction. Digital pictures need to be taken of different experiments and be a related part of the write-up. Illustrations may also be drawn by pupils to accompany an experiment. Journal entries need to pinpoint key vocabulary terms used (See Alien, 2008).

A variety of rich experiences in ongoing science lessons and units of study aids pupils in securing relevant vocabulary terms which are useful presently as well as in the future. Thus, diary entries written by individuals or committees of significant learnings assist pupils to master vocabulary words. Alternating as to who writes the entries stimulates interest and avoids repetition and boredom. *Sequential improvement* in all written work is to be expected, using complete sentences, clarity of ideas and variety in words as well as types of sentences used (See National Research Council, 1996).

Words are powerful and can be use in a plethora of ways. Pertaining to the power of words, Wessler (2008) wrote the following:

> Words are central tools of education. Whether written or spoken, words can elucidate, inform, and inspire. But they can also scare, humiliate and disempower. Degrading slurs, jokes and epithets are pervasive in the hallways, cafeterias,

> buses, locker rooms and even classrooms of middle and high schools everywhere.
>
> A school where degrading language slurs and jokes are widely used and rarely challenged is a place where violence is far more likely to occur. Some students will take the silence of bystanders as license to escalate their behavior from words to harsher words, threats and finally violence. In every instance of violence that I have investigated in schools, first as a hate crime prosecutor and more recently when administrators asked me to help them respond to serious misconduct, I have seen this same process of escalation.

The above quote pinpoints the positive as well as the negative use of words. A positive classroom environment stresses the importance of using words to achieve, grow and develop on the part of students and teachers. A threatening, negative classroom environment hinders achievement of relevant objectives in science. In the curriculum, there are many words which need to be mastered in order to become literate in the academic discipline of science. A carefully chosen video tape shown to students to introduce a new science unit of study may be used to assist pupils to acquire new concepts and words which may be jotted down. At the end of the presentation, pupils may compare their lists by having the teacher print each on the chalkboard, avoiding duplications. Word and vocabulary study are valuable for their own sake as well as for use in school and in society (See Moore and Sampson, 2008).

Concepts studied must be shown as being related to each other in ongoing science units of study. For example, in a unit on simple machines, pupils may study a lever, a pulley, an inclined plane, a screw, a wheel and axle, among others. The science teacher must demonstrate the use of each by having real objects such as a lever, an inclined plane, a pulley, and a screw. Pictorial forms of each simple machine need to be discussed in sequence, followed by pupils seeing the related concept for each in print, large enough for all to see clearly.

The relationship of words need to be printed in a concept web. Pupils might then refer to the concept web to review, rehearse, and assess previous learnings. It is surprising how many pupils will talk to each other about concepts on the word web as well as those on the word wall. Pupils need to think about and apply what has been acquired in order to have adequate background information and increasingly become scientifically literate (Ediger, 2006).

Classroom Environment

The classroom needs to be conducive to pupil learning. Rudeness, inconsiderateness and not caring for each other hinders learner progress. Relevant words and concepts need to be studied by pupils with the level of application involved. A variety of interesting, purposeful procedures must be used in engage pupils in achieving objectives in this area.

REFERENCES

Alien, Rick (2008), "Leveraging Technology to Improve Literacy," *Education Update*, 50(10), 1,3,6.

Ediger, Marlow (2006), "Writing in the Mathematics Curriculum," *Journal of Instructional Psychology*, 33 (2), 120-123.

Ediger, Marlow (2007), "The Substitute Teacher in Reading Instruction," *The SubJournal*, 8 (2), 67-73.

Ediger, Marlow and Rao (2007), School Science Education. New Delhi, India: Discovery Publishing House.

Moore, Leeann and Mary Beth Sampson (2008), "Field Based Teacher Preparation: An Organized Analysis of Enabling Conditions," *Education*, 129 (1), 3-16.

National Research Council (1996), *National Science Education Standards*. Washington, DC: The Academy Press.

Reutzel, D. Ray, *et al.*, (2008), "Scaffolded Silent Reading: A Complement to Guided Repeated Oral Reading That Works!" *The Reading Teacher*, 62 (3), 194-211.

Wessler, Stephen (2008), "Civility Speaks Up," *Educational Leadership*, 66 (1), 44-48.

Zales, Charlotte Ruppe and Connie S. Unger (2008), "The Science and Literacy Framework," *Science and Children*, 46 (3), 42-45.

School Science and the Language Arts

An integrated science curriculum assists pupils to retain learnings better than to separate academic disciplines. Too frequently, science teachers teach each academic discipline as separate entities. However, there is much correlating of science with language, for example which might well be implemented in teaching and learning situations. Thus, reading, writing, and listening skills need developing in order to strengthen the science curriculum.

Improving Science Teaching and Learning Situations

How might the language arts become an integral part of science lessons and units of study? Experimentations need to be the heart of science learnings. For carefully devised science experiments, pupils individually or in committees might well write up the inherent parts of the study. The problem, hypothesis, testing the hypothesis, and making necessary revisions must be written up clearly so that it communicates effectively with other pupils and the teacher. Each part, such as the problem, needs to be written up with complete sentences, possessing proper structure, as in syntax. When readiness exists, pupils might learn about agreement of subject and predicate, as well as correct placement of modifiers such as adjectives and adverbs. The write-ups may be dated and filed for future reference. Knowledge which is used will, no doubt, be retained for a longer period of time as compared to the unused. Recording experiment results emphasizes utilizing knowledge and skills acquired (Ediger and Rao, 2011).

Skills in discussions whether it be the class as a whole or in small groups are always salient in the school setting as well as in the societal arenas. Interaction involves achieving social skills and respecting others. The writer has heard numerous adults say that they never did well in a collaborative endeavor. During the public school years, a plethora of opportunities exist to accomplish selected skills. For instance in a unit on Climate Change, pupils with teacher guidance might discuss the pros and cons emphasized by those who accept and those who are skeptical, in this debate. Criterion for the discussion should include a solid knowledge base of the topic as well as

- adhering to the topic under discussion. Too frequently, people dislike discussions because there is a shift away from the topic. Time can certainly be wasted unless there is merit in making the shift.
- presenting ideas clearly and not interrupting others during the discussion.
- having ideas circulate among participants with no one dominating Ediger and Rao, 2007).

Improvement in achieving these criteria should be a long lasting goal and not immediate perfection. Scientists are able to communicate effectively with others. Quality oral language use must receive its fair share of attention in science lessons and units of study. Using voice inflection, logical thinking, proper stress and pitch of words aids in effective presentation of ideas. Semantics is involved when stressing meaning and clarity in oral communication.

Reading subject matter to comprehend ideas is important. Science has its own unique vocabulary, meaningfully presented, and needs to be acquired by learners to participate well in writing and in committee endeavors. Teaching reading skills in context makes it salient for learners. Thus, the following reading skills need emphasis:

- using context clues. Here, the pupil is not able to identify a word while reading science subject matter. The teacher asks the learner to supply a word which makes sense in relationship to the rest of the words in the sentence or paragraph. Sometimes, a pupil will give an outlandish word which does not make sense. Or, the pupil, provides a meaningful word which is not correct. For the former, the science teacher needs to ask if the provided word by the pupil makes sense. This provides opportunities to come up with a sensible word; for the latter attempt at word recognition, the learner must look at the initial consonant and sound out its related symbol/sound relationship. It might be necessary to sound out other letters to come up with what is correct. Independence is an ultimate goal in correctly recognizing unknown words. Further objectives in reading science content include:

- reading to develop a generalization. Here, the science teacher might ask pupils to state in one sentence what a paragraph or several paragraphs say. It might even be a page or several pages of subject matter whereby learners state in one sentence the meaning obtained.
- reading for a sequence of ideas. This is very important when the pupil is asked what comes first, second, third, and so on, in doing a science experiment.
- reading critically to separate facts from opinions, fantasy from reality and accurate from inaccurate content.

Listening in Ongoing Activities

Listening is sometimes called the forgotten art, and yet individuals do much listening in a given day such as conversing during leisure time. In the science curriculum, there are a plethora of opportunities to achieve skill in listening. The writer has heard numerous times whereby adults wished they were better listeners. In class, much information is lost due to poor listening habits. Sequence in learning is minimized when pupils possess gaps in knowledge which is due to ineffective listening skills. The science teacher might well assist pupils to increase listening skills, by removing distractions such as pupils disturbing each other during discussion time. Unnecessary noises, also, hinder in the listening process. The science teacher, however, does want a relaxed environment in the classroom so that learners can focus on attaining objectives of instruction and not worry due to tension and anxiety. There are salient things for the science teacher to do to encourage improved listening habits:

- have standards posted at the front of the room and refer to them at intervals to remind pupils on good listening habits.
- have pupils periodically review at the end of a lesson selected important ideas presented. This oral review whereby learners in the classroom provide content assists pupils to listen carefully to an ensuing lesson.
- have pupils explain with clarity what had just been emphasized in an ongoing lesson.
- pinpoint to the class, weaknesses in listening which had occurred in a completed lesson. Point to items on the standards chart to stress important behaviors which need implementation.
- from classroom test results, indicate where poor listening habits made for errors in responding.

REFERENCES

Ediger, Marlow and D. Bhaskara Rao (2011), *Essays in Teaching Science*. New Delhi, India : Discovery Publishing House (Ltd.).

Ediger, Marlow and D. Bhaskara Rao (2007), School Science Education. Discovery Publishing House (Ltd.).

Poetry in the Science Curriculum

There are a Plethora of Purposes in Writing in the Science Curriculum

Writing serves a variety of reasons. One purpose is to *use* acquired knowledge. Poetry writing is one approach for the learner to apply what has been learned in ongoing science units of study. Poetry writing has a fascination of its very own. Learners seemingly enjoy writing verse containing rhyme as well as the unrhymed. For each type of poem written, students need to possess readiness factors which include:

- knowledge of characteristics of each kind of poem to be written.
- adequate fluency in writing diverse kinds of poetry.
- functional abilities in spelling.
- positive attitudes toward poetry.
- reading poetry with meaning (Ediger, 2008).

The science teacher then needs to ascertain if students are ready to write poetry in its many forms.

Motivation to Write Poetry

The writer supervised university student teachers for thirty years in the public schools and observed many student teachers and cooperating teachers motivate pupils in diverse kinds of writing activities (See Mesa, *et al.*, 2008).

Student motivation is salient in studying and writing of poems. Developmental appropriate activities need to be in the offing. The science teacher needs to model reading aloud each kind of poem which will be written in sequence. The first kind of poem may be the couplet. Thus, after a science couplet has been read, the teacher may print it for all students to see. A discussion should follow whereby students inductively discover the two lines of verse with ending words rhyming. Generally, the two lines are somewhat equivalent in length. The science teacher may then assist pupils to recall what was studied in the ongoing science unit of study. Acquired facts, concepts and generalizations might well become a significant part of a couplet (See National Research Council, 1996). It is important for the teacher to share a science couplet he/she wrote. The following is an example:

Winter

Cold weather and snow
Help the cold wind blow.

Pupils tend to like experimenting with what has been learned in science in writing couplets. Most like to share orally their individual written couplet with classmates. In this way, pupils review what has been learned and apply these learnings to a new situation. Many student teachers and regular teachers in the public schools, supervised by the writer, had an anthology of children's literature on their desk tops containing interesting poems, related to the present unit being studied.

In sequence, triplets may be studied which contain three lines of rhyme with the lines somewhat uniform in length. Pupils in small groups may desire to write a triplet collectively (Ediger and Rao, 2002). A committee of pupils in a public school wrote the following triplet:

Hail

The spring weather was quite pleasant
Followed by a cooling down of each plant
With pieces of ice from the sky falling at a slant.

Quatrains generally contain four lines of verse with lines one and two as well as lines three and four rhyming or all four lines may rhyme. When pupils posses the needed prerequisites, the science teacher may provide motivational background experiences to stimulate quatrain writing (Ediger and Rao 2007). A quatrain written by a fifth grade pupil contained the following subject matter:

Erosion

With no cover crop for the moisture to hold
A very heavy rain caused soil to erode
Trees and grass may have slowed the runoff bold
Wasted top soil hinders production of future crops to be sold

Pupils should be asked to share, orally, their poems. Each poem read aloud needs to be received by classmates in an atmosphere of respect. Poems might then be posted on a poetry wall for all to read in the classroom. Learning from each other is important (See Pardo, 2004)!

A very interesting kind of poem to write is the limerick. Teacher's anthologies of children's literature contain limericks which should be read aloud in the classroom. Any poem read aloud needs to be read with enthusiasm. Voice inflection with proper stress and pitch of each word needs to be emphasized. The science teacher's voice may be used effectively to secure learner attention. Once pupils have carefully noticed that a limerick contains rhyme in lines one, two, and five, as well as lines three and four rhyming, they need encouragement to apply what has been learned (See Cochran-Smith, 2006). A cooperating teacher wrote and read orally the following model for student contemplation:

Thomas Edison

There once was a great inventor
Who gave the world much light as a vendor
He worked hard until it was perfected
With the incandescent light bulb as he intended
Edison lives forever as our mentor.

Syllabication and Poetry in Science

Selected pupils like to write verse containing a pattern of syllabication, with no expected rhyme. Haiku is a kind of poem built upon five, seven, five syllables for each sequential three lines of poetry. Pupils need to listen to and see several haiku before actually writing a haiku as an ensuing writing experience. A sixth grader wrote the following:

Rocks and minerals
Beautiful, useful, handy
Buildings and fine gems.

The haiku may be extended by adding two lines with seven and seven syllables for each of two lines, making for a tanka. Or, learners may prefer to write a completely new tanka on a different topic studied in science. A student teacher wrote the following which was read aloud to pupils and served as a model for writing:

Tornados, lonely, dark
funnels in the blue rimmed sky
descending from high
very strong winds rushing by
with cone shaped skyward motion.

Selected pupils, when ready, may wish to write free verse, containing no rhyme nor syllables per line. There are a plethora of forms used in writing free verse. The following model was developed and read to students by a cooperating teacher:

Reptiles consist of turtles, crocodiles, alligators and snakes
are cold blooded and sluggish in cold weather
move slowly in the environment
live in water and on land
generally have lungs
eat plants and animals.

The final poem, a diamante, which is diamond shaped should be developed cooperatively by students with teacher guidance.

Soil	(consisting of a single noun)
heavy, moist	(two adjectives)
planting, growing, weeding	(three participles)
Clay, loam, igneous, sedimentary	(four nouns)
plowing, disking, harrowing	(three participles)
dusty, murky	(two adjectives)
dirt	(noun).

In Closing

Values inherent in the writing of poetry in science are numerous. It provides opportunities to put science vocabulary terms to use. Knowledge which is used is less likely to be forgotten. Playing around with science vocabulary assists pupils to be creative when engaged in writing poetry. Creativity is salient in school and in society. Unique, novel ways are needed to come up with innovations in society (See Kennedy, 2008).

REFERENCES

Cochran-Smith, Marilyn (2006), "Ten Promising Trends and Three Big Worries," *Educational Leadership*, 63 (6), 20-25.

Ediger, Marlow (2008), "Leadership in the School Setting," *Education*, 129.

Ediger, Marlow and D. Bhaskara Rao (2002), *Teaching Language Arts Successfully*. New Delhi, India: Discovery Publishing House.

Ediger, Marlow and D. Bhaskara Rao (2007), *School Science Education*. New Delhi, India: Discovery Publishing House (Ltd.).

Kennedy, Mary (2008), "Sorting Out Teaching Quality," *Phi Delta Kappan*, 90 (1), 59-63.

Mesa, Jennifer C., *et.al.* (2008), "The P.O.E.T.R.Y. of Science," *Science and Children*, 46 (3), 36-41.

National Research Council (1996), *National Science Education Standards*. Washington, DC: National Academy Press.

Pardo, Laura (2004), "What Every Teacher Needs to Know About Comprehension," *The Reading Teacher*, 58 (3), 272-284.

Decision-making in the Science Curriculum

There are numerous worthwhile objectives for pupils to achieve in science. Knowledge objectives are salient for learner achievement, but equally important are skills ends. Perhaps, the two kinds of objectives cannot be separated from each other. Knowledge is used when making choices, from among alternative subject matter which might be studied. Then too, knowledge decisions are used to solve problems. Thus, facts, concepts and generalizations are chosen to find solutions.

Being able to make decisions is very useful in school settings where short and more long terms choices are made such as friendships versus possible vocational choices. In the science curriculum, choices might also be stressed in terms of which objectives to pursue, learning opportunities to engage in, as well as choices in assessment procedures, from among others. Ongoing science lessons and units of study provide ample opportunities for decisions making (Ediger and Rao, 2007).

Decision-making in Science

The science teacher needs to be well versed in styles of learning and how to provide for individual differences among learners. Using learning centers is one method to emphasize to encourage pupils in making choices from among alternatives. One or more centers, teacher determined or through teacher/ pupil planning, may then be put into place in a classroom. If one learning center is developed by the science teacher, then enrichment learnings may be stressed. The teacher develops a task card suggesting possibilities for choosing a learning activity. Materials to use are also available at the center. Here, pupils, for example, may choose to make models of prehistoric life from clay or play-dough. Or at a more complex level, depending upon learners readiness, a pupil may choose to do a written report on plants and animals in the Mesozoic Era.

Several learning centers might also be developed. Thus, five or six centers, each containing four tasks listed on a card provide choices for pupils to select and complete individually or in a small group endeavor. In a science unit on changes in the earth's surface, pupils, here, may select to work at the following stations, as examples:

- a hurricane/tornado center whereby pupils may view related video tapes on this topic and do a written/oral report to the class on their findings.
- a soil erosion center indicating the effects of wind/ water on soil. Ways of preventing and minimizing these effects should also be studied with the use of different reference sources such as the internet. Models may be made to show counteractions to prevent soil erosion with the planting of trees and grass.
- drawings might well be completed on causes of earthquakes. Pupils may use science encyclopedias, among other reference sources, to secure necessary information with the results posted on the classroom bulletin board (See Blough and Schwartz, 1984).

It was noticed by the authors when supervising student teachers in the public schools that a few teachers used learning centers for an entire science unit of study. Others used a few centers to supplement the regular science curriculum whereas some used one center for enrichment purposes. When making decisions in using a learning centers procedure, the following need consideration:

- how well pupils are learning when using this approach. Do they achieve objectives well in a decision-making procedure of learning?
- are pupils responsible individuals in an informal approach to learning?
- do pupils use the methods the of science when participating in decision-making in doing science activities and experiences?
- are learners showing respect and acceptance of others? (See Booker, 2008).

Decision-making by pupils may also be stressed when carefully chosen science textbooks are used as a guide for lessons and units of study taught. Thus within a lesson, pupils might identify a problem for solving. The problems is relevant and must be clearly stated so it can be solved. Deliberation is necessary. An hypothesis is developed as a tentative answer to the identified problem. Various reference sources are used to gather information to test the tentative hypothesis.

Projects may also be chosen as a result of pupils being engaged in reading/discussing ideas from the basal science textbook. The project may involve individual or committee work such as making models, taking an excursion and summarizing its findings, as well as constructing objects and items related directly to the ongoing unit of study (See National Research Council, 1996).

Discussion groups may also be formed whereby peers gather information and discuss alternative forms of energy such as solar, geothermal and wind. A detailed set of conclusions may be drawn up to evaluate the quality of the findings/discussion. In committee work, it is important for all to participate and no one dominate in the different interactions. Ideas need to be stated clearly as individuals participate.

Reading across the curriculum might truly be stressed when basal textbooks are used in science teaching and learning. When reading content, pupils may be assisted in phonics, use of context clues, onset and rimes in word pronunciation, as well as prefixes and suffixes in identification of words (Ediger, 1996).

Learnings may certainly be extended when basals are used. Library book and internet sources may be integrated into the ongoing unit of study when basal science texts are utilized. Extended learnings are emphasized when:

- it adds to meaningful science facts, concepts and generalizations.
- it assists pupils to develop indepth interests in science through problem solving, project methods and discussions.
- it provides for individual differences such as abilities and talents of learners.
- it varies the kinds of learning opportunities provided for pupils in he classroom setting.

Toward the other end of the continuum in a more formal science curriculum, the teacher may select science objectives which are measurably stated for pupils to attain. These may come from mandated objectives on the state level. The objectives deal with knowledge ends largely. The objectives are precisely written and pupils do/do not achieve them as a result of teaching. Learning activities are then aligned with the stated objectives. Test results may be machine scored and one correct answer for each multiple choice test item is possible. Each pupil's results are indicated numerically as in percentiles, standard deviations and grade equivalents. Unless the teacher invites, there is little leeway to emphasize questions from learners, discussion groups and project development (See Beckstead, 2008).

Testing is a major way of determining what pupils have learned in a formal approach of teaching. With test scores from pupil test results, the teacher may notice how well learners are achiving. With mandated tests, the results from testing of different classrooms and schools, comparisons can be made to notice the quality of achievement. Are pupils doing better than previously? Teachers might well be held accountable for these test resuts. Accountability is then being emphasized. Pertaining to accountability, Johnson and Bonaiuto (2009) wrote the following:

> Accountability is the catalyst that drives educational progress. But if accountability does not grow out of a local context, with roots in what the community values, it loses meaning.

Too frequently, educators rely on test scores as the primary measure of how well a school is doing. Externally mandated data rather than community priorities shape the public conversation about education. Newspapers publish school rankings, parents look to see how their child stacks up and teachers are able to handle community pressures centered on test scores with no other measure as a balance.

There are numerous methods of evaluation, in addition to testing, which may be used to ascertain learner achievement and progress. These include:

- teacher observation. He/she may observe how well pupils interact with each other in committee work such as staying on task and respecting each other.
- anecdotal records. The science teacher records and dates specific observations made as in pupils doing a project such as making a model solar collector. Accuracy, cooperation, neatness and acceptance of others are important observations to make. Interviews with pupils also provide information for anecdotal records.
- self evaluation. Here, pupils may respond with ratings on a five point scale to such items as relies upon the self for task completion, interacts well with others and assists others as needed.

REFERENCES

Beckstead, Larissa (2008), "Scientific Journals," *Science and Children*, 46 (3), 22-26.

Booker, Keonya (2008), "The Role of Peers and Instructors in Establishing a Classroom Community," *Journal of Instructional Psychology*, 35 (1), 12-16.

Blough Glenn and Julius Schwartz (1984), *Elementary School Science and How to Teach It*. New York: CBS Publishing Company.

Ediger, Marlow (1996), "Activity Centered Versus Subject Centered Curriculum," *The Educational Review*, 102 (1), 17-20.

Ediger, Marlow and Digmurti Bhaskarao Rao (2007) *School Science Education*. New Delhi, India: Discovery Publishing House.

Johnson, George and Susan Bonaiuto (2009), "Accountability With Roots," *Educational Leadership*, 66 (4), 26-29.

National Research Council (1996). National Science Education Standards. Washington, DC: Academy Press.

More Emphasis upon Science needed in the School Curriculum

A Headline in NSTA Reports (National Science Teachers Association, 2009) Stated that 'U.S. Students are Static in Science'. Thus, the 2007 Trends in International Mathematics and Science Study (TIMMS), the United States ranked sixth among fourth graders and and tenth among eighth graders, internationally, in science achievement. The article goes on to say that the No Child Left Behind (NCLB) law of 2002 has distracted from science teaching with its required emphasis upon reading and upon mathematics instruction. NCLB stresses pupils needing to pass mandated tests in reading and in mathematics in grades three through eight in order to be promoted to the next higher grade level. Problems in achieving Adequate Yearly Progress (AYP) has also furthered the emphasis upon reading and mathematics instruction.

This has made for situations in schools whereby teachers are to focus upon what will possibly be covered in reading and mathematics on NCLB mandated tests. Selected schools even reported in journal articles that principals advocated to teach only on what will be tested. The scope of the curriculum has then indeed been narrowed. Science mandated testing by NCLB was included in a belated manner in the 2008-2009 school year. This has made for greatly minimizing the importance of teaching science, especially in the elementary and middle school years. Learnings are sequential and previous experiences in science assist in pupils developing increasingly complex science concepts and generalizations (Ediger and Rao, 2007).

Science for All Pupils in the School Curriculum

Individual live in a scientific world. Science has brought tremendous achievements for the human condition such as continual improvement in medical practices, manual labor saving devices, transportation, communication and safety in food products consumed, among others. The natural world may create havocs such as earthquakes, mud slides, floods, ice storms, drought, tornados/hurricanes, soil erosion and hail. The latter ruin farm crops and cause heavy expenses for building repairs, in general. It has been difficult to deal with losses from these affects, but human beings need to rebuild and redo while attempting to minimize causes for these losses. Vital needed improvements include having underground cable to avoid electrical problems from ice storms; people do depend upon electricity for heat and survival in homes across the nation. Other salient needs include:

- quality health care available to all in society, regardless of income levels.
- safe, updated school buildings with good teachers for each pupil.
- road and bridge repairs for safety in travel and transportation.
- federal moneys available to assist students to go to and graduate from college or technical school.
- safe, affordable housing for each person.
- job market which has necessary work with adequate salaries for workers.
- mass transit system providing transportation at a reasonable cost to individuals (Ediger, 2008).

In each of the above situations and ideals, science has an important role to play which makes it a necessity to provide a quality science curriculum for each pupil. A starting point here would be to evaluate if science instruction is receiving its fair share of school time. Adequate time is needed to provide for an effective science curriculum. To use the allotted time efficiently, pupils must experience vital objectives to achieve, be it mandated or locally developed. The following objectives are highly important to achieve by pupils:

- objective, careful observers of science phenomenon.
- critical and creative thinking abilities, as well as problem-solving skills.
- metacognition skills to reflect upon what has been learned.
- doing quality projects, evaluated in terms of desired criteria.
- being able to carryout science experiments to evaluate information.
- showing learnings acquired through graphs, charts and tables.
- reading science content with meaning and understanding.
- listening with a variety of purposes involved (See Parker, 2001).

The list could go on to include using inferential thinking, and developing good attitudes toward science learnings in general, such as pupils being curious pertaining to the natural environment. Updating teacher knowledge and skills is a continuous concern. Each school needs to possess a library for teachers to house teacher education science textbooks and journals, as well as a reputable daily newspaper/newsmagazine which contain accounts on current events involving noteworthy science happenings (floods and tornados, for example). There should be a table and comfortable chairs, suitable for reading activities. Science teachers need to be encouraged to use the science library to promote inservice growth (See Zales and Linger, 2008).

Also, teachers should be challenged to take graduate courses in science eduction. Taking courses online or at an approved university increases chances for teacher growth in teaching science. There are always possibilities of doing an independent study in providing for pupil individual differences in teaching learners. The point remains that science education needs to be emphasized.

Grade level teacher discussion groups should be held to share ideas on improving instruction. New ideas for teaching may be tried out in the classroom and results reported back to the discussion group. From these diverse inservice education approaches, teachers may wish to provide suggestions for a quality workshop whereby all participants benefit from its proceedings. Thus, a theme might be chosen and a large group session held to select problem areas in science teaching. From these identified problem areas, committees may be formed to work in the direction of solving respective problems in science instruction. Suggestions for teaching an innovation should provide opportunities for teaching science in the classroom. Participants at the workshop need to be informed of these outcomes. One salient area of instruction is in doing science experiments safely in the classroom. One variable alone needs to be tested in an experiment for pupils. The carefully designed experiment needs to stress an hypothesis to be tested. As a result of testing, the hypothesis may be modified, revised, or left as is. The methods of science must be stressed in experimentation. Teachers need to appraise the quality of the workshop in terms of desired criteria such as:

- was the workshop beneficial to improve instruction?
- did you try out innovative ideas in your classroom?
- how did pupils in your classroom benefit from the ideals emphasized in the workshop?
- did you feel free to ask questions of consultants in the workshop? (See National Research Council, 1996).

Evaluation results may be tabulated and used for future inservice education endeavors. The purpose of workshops is to assist teachers to provide quality objectives, learning opportunities and evaluation procedures in teaching and learning situations. The science curriculum must be assessed and updated periodically. Pupils individually need to achieve as much as possible in science. Individual differences must be provided for.

Demonstration teaching is another facet and procedure of curriculum improvement in science. Who might do the demonstration teaching? Attempts must be made to identify science teachers, presently teaching or retirees, to do quality demonstration teaching in science. Science education professors from a nearby university may be willing to demonstrate how to teach selected concepts and generalizations in science. Carefully chosen video-tapes, also, might well provide models for science teaching. Methods stressed should assist pupils of all achievement levels to attain vital objectives of instruction. The point is that there are a plethora of ways to improve science teaching. The science supervisor, too, needs to appraise teaching quality in the classroom in order to help pupils attain more optimally. He/she may assess science teachers in the following areas:

- providing meaningful learning activities so that pupils understand what was taught.
- engaging pupils in ongoing activities and experiences to encourage interest in learning.
- assisting pupils to perceive purpose in ongoing science lessons and units of study.
- encouraging pupil curiosity in science.
- helping pupils to reflect upon what was learned to emphasize retention of learnings acquired.
- guiding pupils to use the internet to extend achieved learnings (See Smolleck, 2007).

To aid pupils in reading science content, such as from the basal textbook, the teacher needs to assist pupils in securing background information for the ensuing activity. Thus, the science teacher needs to discuss relevant illustrations directly related to the subject matter to be read. Questions raised here, by pupils, might well be answered during/from the reading experience. Prior to reading, pupils need to see the new words, enlarged on a screen, projected from a computer. Each word must be highlighted as it is being identified. Meaning must be attached to each word as used in context in the basal textbook in science. Pupils should then be able to comprehend ideas in context. Followup experiences from textbook reading might include:

- discussing answers to questions indepth.
- identifying a problem area and finding a related solution.
- doing a mural or diorama.
- constructing a model.
- working cooperatively on a project.
- writing a report of major ideas read.

The basal textbook activity may be extended by having pupils read for information on additional self selected science content. Thus, the science teacher may choose library books to be housed at a learning center in the classroom. The library books are on different topics in science and are at diverse reading levels to provide for individual learners. Each pupil may choose a library book to read. Decision-making is then involved. During the silent reading time, the science teacher may ask pupils individually a few questions along the way to assess comprehension and time on task. Assistance also must be provided to pupils who need help in word recognition. The reading experience needs to flow as seamless as possible in order that pupils might gain vital facts, concepts and generalizations in science (See Rice, 2002).

In Closing

Time needs to be used wisely in teaching science. Pupils need to achieve worthwhile objectives in each unit of study. However, pupils do need time to reflect upon what has been learned indepth. Pertaining to wasted school time, Olson (2008) wrote:

Some procedures will always be necessary, but many can be streamlined or omitted. Transitions between rooms, subjects and breaks are prime spots where time can be saved. Get students started quickly when they return to the room. Take attendance while students are working on an academic task. When possible, show relevant clips of videos rather than the entire program. Have smooth procedures for collecting and distributing paperwork. Decide if "free time" or "homework time" at the end of the day is worth the cost to your science programs. Evan a few minutes add up to a significant amount of time over the course of the school year.

REFERENCES

Ediger, Marlow and Digumarti Bhaskara Rao (2007) *School Science Education*. New Delhi, India: Discovery Publishing House.

Ediger, Marlow (2008), "The School and Students in Society," *Journal of Instructional Psychology*, 35 (3), 260-264.

National Research Council (NRC). National Science Education Standards (1996), Washington, DC.

National Science Teachers Association (2009), *NSTA Reports*. Arlington, Virginia: The Association.

Olson, Joanne K. (2008), "Methods and Strategies," *Science and Children*, 46 (3), 52-53.

Parker, Walter (2001), Social Studies in Elementary Education. Upper Saddle River, New Jersey: Prentice Hall, Inc.

Rice, D. C. (2002), "Using Trade Books in Teaching Elementary School Science," *The Reading Teacher*, 55 (6), 552-565.

Smolleck, L.D. (2007), "Science in the Elementary School Classroom-Post NCLB," *Teachers College Record*.

Zales, Charlotte Rappe and Connie S. Linger (2008), "The Science and Literacy Framework," *Science and Children*, 46 (3), 42-45.

Parent/Teacher Conferences and the Science Curriculum

In an increasingly complex society, all pupils need to possess high levels of literacy in science. The news media is filled with items pertaining to the natural world such ad hurricanes, tornados, earthquakes, tsunamis, drought, floods and mudslides, among others. Science has provided the lay public with modern technology to make life easier and more convenient. Modern appliances, cooling and heating systems, means of transportation and processes in food preservation, among others, have used principles of science to improve society. The world of science needs to be used to improve society and the human condition. It can also be used for destructive purposes. Knowledgeable persons need to make rational decisions based on the solving of problems in terms of which direction science and technology may move forward (Ediger and Rao, 2007).

Parents need to be well-informed of their offspring's progress in science learnings. Parent/teacher conferences might well assist parents to understand pupil achievement more fully. These conferences need to follow selected criteria. There needs to be respect among participants in order for quality communication to occur. Rudeness and intimidation have no roles to play in a conference. Participants need to feel free to ask questions and make comments pertaining to the child's progress in science. Each must seek to learn as much as possible about how well the learner is achieving in ongoing science lessons and units of study (See National Science Teachers Association, 2001).

The science teacher needs to be well prepared for the conference and parents, too, need to identify questions and problems involving the offspring's progress. This provides a setting for a profitable conference.

What should the science teacher have available for the parent/teacher conference to show parents in terms of learner products? If a portfolio has been kept, this would make for a device to show progress in science achievement. Among others, the science portfolio will usually contain the following representations of a pupil's work:

- written book reports of science library books read
- digital pictures of science experiments and committee work engaged in
- summaries of science experiments and demonstrations
- sample pages from science journals and diaries kept.

From the above items, parents may ask questions of the science teacher such as the following:

- Is the pupil making adequate progress overall in science?
- What can we do at home to assist the child to improve in achievement?
- Might selected science experiments be done at home with the child?
- How can the learner be assisted in reading and writing in science?
- How may the use of computers assist pupil progress (See Ediger 1990)?

Each of the above needs to be discussed in depth with the intent of assisting the child to improve in science knowledge, skills and attitudes. There needs to be an agreement of what the home and school will do to help the pupil achieve more optimally. The science teacher needs to secure relevant information from parents to assist the child in future science learnings. Information such as the following is vital for the science teacher to guide pupil progress:

- does the child ask interesting questions involving science? Science is everywhere and the child needs to be aware of this. Pupils have asked why the water level goes down in the living room aquarium containing gold fish, or what happens when a mud puddle becomes dry in summer time.
- do you visit science museums, if available, in your area? The point is to visit interesting places with the child where science learnings are stimulated. Most cities have museums where science learning is stressed. A traveling display of dinosaurs in a small university museum captured the interests of many students. Seeing the skeletal remains of the brontosaurs, the diplodocus, the stegosaurs, among others, is fascinating to all. Parents should learn together with their children. Supon (2006) wrote the following pertaining to the use of digital cameras to film important phenomenon:

  Digital camera use increases analytical skills and can be used as a means of assessing student performance. Having students know what high quality performance is can effectively be documented through photographs. When students recognize similarities and differences of their performance through photos, students become reflective and effective with self-assessment. This process increases performance.
- do you read science library books together and discuss their contents? A good collection of science books is important in the home setting. Library books may be checked out free from the school and city library. Science literacy is for all. Pertaining to science literacy, Zales and Unger (2008) wrote the following:

  Reading captivating stories - both fiction and non-fiction - provide enjoyment for students, through both the text and the illustrations. Carefully selected trade books can introduce science concepts, develop background knowledge, reinforce hands-on lessons, support process skills and at the same time enhance science literacy process skills. They can also provide inspiration and structure for integrated science and literacy lessons.

Parent-teacher conferences may be carried out by using a variety of approaches. Face to face interaction, in a caring manner, is, probably, the best procedure. However, there are additional procedures such as telephone calls, e-mail and letter writing.

In Conclusion

There are key concepts to emphasize in the science curriculum. The following are salient:

- **problem solving.** This involves critical and creative thinking to secure answers to questions involving dilemmas.
- **objectivity.** Students are to think and observe as things really are, without personal biases and prejudices.
- **inquiry learning.** Students need to learn by discovery methods.
- **key structural content in science subject matter.** These are major generalizations, concepts and facts, vital in academic science learning.
- **use of science equipment.** Here, students need to make applicable the methods of science by using modern technology.

REFERENCES

Ediger, Marlow (1990), *Role of Philosophy in Teaching Science*, Paideia, Published by the Polish Academy of Science, Warsaw, Poland, pp. 242-246.

Ediger, Marlow and Digumarti Bhaskara Rao (2007), *School Science Education*. New Delhi, India: Discovery Publishing House.

National Science Teachers Association (2001), *Classroom Assessments and the National Education Standards*. Washington DC: NSTA.

Supon, Viola (2006), "Using Digital Cameras for Multidimensional Learning," *Journal of Instructional Psychology*, 33 (1), 154-156.

Zales, Charlotte Rappe, and Connie S. Unger (2008), "The Science and Literacy Framework," *Science and Children*, 46 (3), 42-45.

School Science and the Integrated Curriculum

Science can well be integrated into the other academic areas in the school setting. There are numerous units of study which may focus on science as the core and additional curriculum endeavors reflecting these structural ideas. Integration of subject matter assists pupils to relate ideas and retain leanings for a longer period of time than would otherwise be the case, Careful planning by the science teacher or teaching team might well turn into highly productive units of study. Objectives in common core state standards (CCSS) might well be brought into these ensuing units. Relevancy is an important concept to stress throughout the planning period since subject matter and skills must be useful in school and in society. Trivia and the unimportant need to be omitted and then stress what is salient.

Relating Academic Disciplines in Science

Key, structural ideas need to be identified which provide a framework for each science unit of study. This takes time and must be given adequate effort in order to have learners achieve these major objectives of instruction. Relevancy is salient here in that there is much to learn and important subject matter must be emphasized. Subordinate ideas also need identification and nurturing in the ensuing activities. Inquiry methods of teaching might then be utilized to assist learners to attain the selected structural and subordinate content. Inquiry methods are opposite of rote learning, memorization and lecture. Rather, pupils are to discover these ideas with the use of a variety of learning experiences, including the following:

- **Experimentation:** A well-designed set of materials, carefully presented and used in an experiment for all to see clearly, presents opportunities for pupils to hypothesize as to its outcomes (Ediger and Rao, 2011). The hypotheses may be recorded and are to be considered as educated guesses. Each hypothesis needs to be evaluated with the utilization of a variety of reference sources. History may be brought, from the social studies, which stresses the work of earlier scientists emphasizing scientific methods and processes such as Galileo, Francis Bacon and William Harvey.
- **Excursions:** These may be taken on the school grounds to observe evaporation in a mud puddle. This may be observed over a two/three day period of time. Other possibilities for excursions include the following:
- **Soil erosion:** Many school grounds have erosion of the soil and also means of prevention such as seeding grass, planting trees and terraces.

  Pupils in the class-room have a plethora of opportunities in reading library books pertaining to plant and animal life. These reading and language arts experiences might well become an integral part of oral communication in science lessons and units of study. Standards for discussions include staying on the topic, respecting others and presenting ideas clearly.

Third, Scientists are good writers of assembled information including that from experimentation as well as from excursions. There are additionally a plethora of examples of pupils doing written work in the science curriculum which include:

- writing a summary of a library book dealing with an aspect of science.
- engaging in problem solving and writing up the salient parts of the problem, such as in, "What a tsunami?"

- keeping a written record of current event items in science occurrences covering a specified interval of time. Current events such as the following are somewhat continuous and relevant in the media: hurricanes and tornados, mudslides, floods, drought and volcanic eruptions.
- doing a study and writing up the contents on topics including global warming and evolution.
- completing an outline in giving an oral class presentation on Charles Darwin, Thomas Huxley, among other scientists.

Fourth, pupils may engage in project methods of instruction. A hands on approach is stressed here with learners sequencing their own individual endeavors. Careful selection of the project with appropriate standards of procedure must be in the offing. Each is to be In of Heavy pupil involvement and collaborative endeavors are generally emphasized. Each project needs to be evaluated in terms of being placed in a local school science fair exhibition. A learning by doing approaches is being stressed in doing a project. Pupils are responsible for their own progress, with teacher guidance, in planning, carrying out the plans and developing criteria to use in the assessment process.

Fifth reading of science content is highly valuable for pupils. Fluency in reading and comprehension aids the pupil in understanding ensuing subject matter. Word recognition enters in to the discussion. If a learner does not identify a word in print, the teacher or a student needs to pronounce correctly the unknown. To become independent in word identification, the teacher needs to ask, "What word fits in and makes sense with the other words in the sentence?" An added clue may enter in if the pupil responds incorrectly with the learner looking at the first letter, generally a consonant and sounding out that letter as well as making sense in the sentence. The teacher must look at patterns of incorrect responses when evaluating word identification problems of pupil. This provides information to the teacher of which kinds of reading errors need attention in the classroom.

Comprehension strategies need attention such as reading for:

- Salient facts and vocabulary development.
- the main idea or major generalization with supporting ideas for each.
- analysis of subject matter in separating accurate from inaccurate content.
- purposes of creative thinking in coming up with unique, novel ideas. Originality of ideas is salient in being innovative and productive.

In closing

There are a plethora of variables to analyze and synthesize when developing a quality science curriculum. Science teachers and supervisors need to spend an adequate amount of time in unit and lesson construction in order to aid each pupil to achieve more optimally.

REFERENCES

Ediger, Marlow and D. Bhaskara Rao (2011), *Essays on Science Curriculum*, New Delhi, India: Discovery Publishing House.

Motivating Students in the Science Curriculum

Motivating students to learn is continually important in teaching and learning situations, science being no exception. Motivated students are easier to teach and do achieve more optimally. The science teacher must select relevant objectives for pupils to attain. There needs to be balance among knowledge, skills and attitudinal objectives. Each is salient. Knowledge ends pertain to vital science facts, concepts and generalizations for learners to acquire, inductively as well as deductively. Skills emphasize using content from the knowledge objectives. Attitudinal ends are on outgrowth of learning activities stressed for pupils in achieving the desired knowledge and skills objectives.

Factors involved in Motivating Pupils

There are a plethora of factors involved in motivation. First, pupils need to be engaged in an ongoing learning experience. In a science unit on classification of animals, pupils may observe fish in the classroom aquarium. Many characteristics of fish may be noticed such as how they move, how they breathe and stay under water and what they eat. Illustrations shown further clarifies concepts pertaining to fish. Motivated pupils secure much knowledge from observations made. Questions raised and discussions held further elaborate on vital ideas pertaining to fish. Meticulous observations made objectively are characteristics of a good scientist! A chart may be developed of observations made, showing characteristics of vertebrates classified as fish. To branch out for further learning activities, pupils might be guided to develop a scrapbook, individually or in a committee, of different kinds of fish and their accompanying pictures. Reading science subject matter is another good way to attain necessary information. All experiences need to be challenging and success oriented (Ediger and Rao, 2003).

Second, pupils need to experience background information to understand new learnings. In classifying a second category of vertebrates, pupils should study amphibians. During the spring months, pupils might study tadpoles swimming in a jar. As they mature, tadpoles become more like frogs. Direct observation, again, is salient to notice these changes in time. Pupils should keep a journal of changes occurring from tadpoles in water to frogs on land. Illustrations drawn by pupils should accompany the respective write-up. The internet should be used to gather information, in depth, pertaining to amphibians, to check direct observations made. Library book content may provide further information on amphibians (See Cuniff and McMillen, 1996).

Third, learners need to study the category of reptiles. These can be quite diverse in their representation and include snakes, turtles, alligators and crocodiles. To become and remain motivated, pupils must attach meaning and understand what is taught and learned. A power point presentation may pin-point specific features for each reptile named above and assist in making learnings meaningful. Individually, or in committees, pupils may list features which distinguish reptiles from amphibians and fish. Likenesses also need to be explored such as being cold-blooded. The listings need to be compared and accurate conclusions drawn. A variety of reference sources may be used to corroborate or refute findings. Objectivity is a key element in learning (See Horejsi 2003).

Fourth, birds provide a fourth category of invertebrates. Here, the science teacher may have pupils look outdoors to see different kinds of birds. A bird feeder located outside the classroom window attracts blue jays, cardinals, sparrows and finches. Pupils tend to be fascinated with birds in the out of doors. They notice and discuss their characteristics. Pupils are interested in knowing that this is the first category of vertebrates which are warm blooded and whose body temperature is much higher than that of human beings. During the school year, they notice which birds migrate such as robins. Pupils learn which birds eat seeds, insects, or both kinds of feed. A comparison chart was developed by separate committees to show how birds differ from reptiles, frogs, and fish. A video tape was then played showing these comparisons and pupils could check their charted hypotheses from that in the video tape. A lively discussion followed pertaining vertebrates read about pertaining to other regions in the world. The duck billed platypus of Australia has characteristics of both birds and mammals. Pupils need to think critically when separating these categories and why they possess similarities and differences. Critical thinking is a major objective in teaching science (See National Research Council, 1996).

Next, mammals need to be studied in ongoing lessons and in a unit of study, together with other vertebrates. Many children have a pet cat or dog as a source of information. The basal text contains illustrations and subject matter on diverse mammals, as well as other categories of vertebrates. The illustrations need to be studied to provide pupils with background information for reading the ensuing content. The new words to be encountered may be printed on the chalkboard for pupil viewing and discussing. They might also be shown on a screen projected by a computer. The new words may then be identified by pupils when reading the assigned subject matter. Readiness for reading by possessing background information and by being able to identify the new words in print is salient. Pupils will raise questions prior to the reading activity on mammals. These questions may be printed on a flip chart for pupils to secure needed information while reading. The new words may also be printed on a word wall for future reference. Answers to questions might well be a followup activity. The teacher may identify additional questions and problems for discussion. Problems take time in identifying an hypothesis to be tested with the use of additional reference sources for further study and analysis (See Blough and Schwartz 1984).

When reading science content, pupils need to *monitor* their comprehension individually to notice if meaning and understanding is occurring and not word calling only. By rehearsing subject matter read, pupils realize if comprehension is occurring. Two pupils reading the same content from the basal may listen to each other explain subject matter read. In this way, both become more conscious of content comprehended. *Metacognitive* strategies, acquired by pupils, helps learners to reflect upon what has been read to ascertain if:

- ideas read possessed clarity.
- content is nebulous and needs more indepth study.
- improved reading strategies might be used, if so which ones?
- different word attack skills need to be used.
- critical thought needs to be used pertaining to a conclusion reached.
- creative thinking is necessary to explore novel ideas (See Fitzburgh, 2006).

Creative thinking stresses pupils coming up with unique ideas in ongoing discussions. Poetry, in particular emphasizes originality of thought and making novel comparisons. Science content studied may be transposed into different kinds of verse written by pupils. In this way, pupils use science subject matter studied. Thus, pupils need to attach meaning to and write free verse:

* fish breathe through gills, not lungs
use the tail and fins to propel motion
live in water, not on land
swim rapidly to secure food and avoid enemies
lay eggs to provide offspring.

* rhymed verse may include a quatrain, containing four lines with alternate lines of rhyme:

amphibians live part of their lives in water
they also live on land
amphibians begin life with gills, then lungs later
and may live on sand.

Additional kinds of rhyme include couplets (two lines of rhymed verse); triplets with three lines of rhymed verse; and limericks whereby lines one, two and five rhyme with lines three and four rhyming.

* poetry containing a selected number of syllables per line, such as haiku with its five, seven, five progression of syllables per line:

Cold blooded turtles
They live on both land and sea
Their young hatch from eggs.

Many pupils, when ready, like to experiment with writing different kinds of poetry (Tiedt, 1982). They find it fascinating to put science knowledge to use in a creative manner and this should aid in retention of subject matter. There are a variety of ways to use content learned in addition to those discussed previously and include the following:

- self-evaluation of subject matter acquired.
- teacher evaluation of pupil achievement, such as in anecdotal statements.
- charts developed to show the progression of stages in each category of vertebrates.
- scrapbooks containing illustrations of each category of vertebrates with vital subject matter explaining each.
- making models of vertebrates from paper mache[1] and/ or paper toweling of fish, snakes, turtles, birds and mammals. When supervising university student teachers, the writer noticed these kinds of models made by sixth graders and then suspended with string from the classroom ceiling.
- developing an individual portfolio (See Bowers, 2005).

As pupils make these models, they ask questions about vertebrates and seek more related information. *Motivation* to learn is then indeed high!

REFERENCES

Blough, Glenn O. and Julius Schwartz (1984), *Elementary School Science and How to Teach It*. New York: CBS College Publishing.

Bowers, Susan P. (2005), "The Portfolio Process: Questions for Implementation and Practice," College Student Journal, 39 (4), 753-758.

Cuniff, Patricia A. and Janet K. McMillen (1996), "Field Studies," *The Science Teacher*, 63: 51.

Ediger, Marlow, and D. Bhaskara Rao (2003), *Teaching Science in Elementary School*, New Delhi, India: Discovery Publishing House.

Fitzburgh, Will (2006), "Where's the Content?" *Educational Leadership*, 64 (2), 42-47.

Horejsi, Martin (2003), "Making Technology Inclusive," *Science and Children*, 41 (3), 20-24.

National Research Council (1996), *National Science Education Standards*. Washington, DC: National Academy Press.

Tiedt, Iris M. (1982), *The Language Arts Handbook*. Prentice-Hall, Inc., Engjewood Cliffs, New Jersey.

Science Fairs and the Student

Developing a project for a science fair can be highly interesting as well as purposeful for the learner. When supervising university student teachers in the public schools, the writer has noticed much enthusiasm shown by students in doing individual and committee projects in science. Sometimes, these projects have been shown at a local science fair in the school district. This makes it possible for all students to participate. It should be voluntary, not a requirement, to participate. Some students do need *encouragement* to complete a science project and complete it jn time for showing. People at these science fairs tend to ask a plethora of questions pertaining to these projects, making it necessary for learners to be well prepared to provide quality answers as well as secure additional information for further indepth study (Ediger, 1996).

Criteria for Project Development

There are salient factors for students to consider when developing a project, generally from an ongoing science unit of study. Thus, students should perceive a purpose. The purpose should ideally come from the student. Having parental involvement is good since this may well serve as a motivator, but the purpose as well as planning and carrying out the plans should be the role of the student. Purposes should be discussed indepth with the science teacher. Relevancy must be considered in thinking about a purpose for project development. Thus, the science fair project must be perceived as being salient. Which purposes may be considered important when developing a science fair project, pertaining to an ongoing unit of study, "The Changing and Sustainable Surface of the Earth?"

- making a model volcano from plaster of Paris and using tempera paint to outline specific features. Models may also be made of mudslides, watersheds, soil erosion, flood waters to contain flood waters, among others.
- developing a model scene to prevent soil erosion with terraces, trees, strip cropping and grass.
- doing a model solar unit together with a listing and illustrations of pollution in its diverse forms from different energy sources.
- making a detailed set of drawings on clean, renewable sources of energy such as wind power, solar panels on homes, geothermal, as well as other sustainable and clean sources of energy (Ediger, 2000).

Projects developed need to possess quality standards of accuracy, neatness and thoroughness. Each project must possess related statements on the purpose of the project, the involved planning, the carrying out of the plans and how each was evaluated with the accompanying desired criteria.

Each project needs to be developmentally appropriate for the involved student. Projects may be developed individually or within a committee of learners. Gathering and appraising relevant information from a variety of reference sources is vital to the project being developed. The student needs to be highly knowledgeable of his/her project. Those observing the projects at the science fair, no doubt, will tend to ask many related questions and the developer needs to be ready to answer questions proficiently. As a judge at many school science fairs, the writer asked the developers of each item judged, the following questions, as an example:

- where did you get the ideas from in developing your project?

- did you work individually on this project or were others involved?
- which reference sources and what information did you use to complete your project?
- how would you judge the quality of your project? Why do you think so?
- what, if anything, would you do differently next time? (See National Research Council, 1996).

Pictures taken of student projects may become excellent parts of a portfolio for the evaluation of learner progress as well as for newspaper write-ups of science fair entries. Pertaining to the use of digital cameras, Supon (2006) wrote the following positive uses:

> Digital camera use increases analytical skills and can be used as a means of assessing student performance. Having students know what high quality is can effectively be documented through photographs. When students recognize similarities and differences of their performance through photos, students become reflective and effective with self assessment. This process increases better performance, performance.

It is recognized that digital cameras have a definite impact in today's classroom. With effective usage, multidimensional learning opportunities occur for students.

Dewey's point abut the destructive power of schools should make us ask ourselves some fundamental questions. What is the purpose of school? What dispositions about learning, reading, school, the world, and the self do we want to cultivate? Ask young children why they go to school. You will hear nothing about joy (Wolk, 2008). Wolk goes on to analyze the concept of joy in school for students:

- Find the pleasure in learning
- Give students choice
- Let students create things
- Show off student work

- Take time to tinker
- Make school space inviting
- Get outside (the classroom)
- Read good books
- Transform assessment.

Too frequently, students find learning as being drudgery as well as being boring. Science fairs might well replace these feelings with doing things which bring satisfaction and self esteem. Students own the project being contemplated and completed. By providing opportunities for decision making, learners are engaged in doing what is salient presently in school as well as throughout life in society. The choice might well stressing creative endeavors. Novelty and uniqueness are inherent. There are times, too, for students to share what has been completed with others. Here, the student may explain and answer questions of the questioner. Critical thinking may be a part of the learnings experienced in securing information related directly to queries. By providing time for project development, students experiment with new procedures and approaches. A variety of materials need to be available in the classroom to reward creative work of learners working on science projects. Excursions might also be necessary to motivate students to identify possible concepts for project work. Traditional methods of learning should not be minimized such as reading experiences to obtain ideas for science fair projects. Library books as well as the basal science textbook may be used as reference sources (See Zales and Unger, 2008). Innovative methods of evaluation might well include use of portfolios to show student progress. Within the portfolio, representative student work in science needs to be incorporated such as:

- written science book reports revealing salient concepts and generalizations secured.
- digital camera photos of science experiments and science projects developed.

- science journals and diaries kept on classroom science lessons and units of study experienced.
- field trips and excursions made, directly related and integral to subject matter studied.

The portfolio may be bound and shown as a science fair project. It must be appealing and gain parental and audience attention! Criteria for its development and assessment need to be in the offing. Transforming assessment, from testing to innovative approaches, is important (Ediger, 2006).

REFERENCES

Ediger, Marlow (1996), "Evaluation of Pupil Achievement, *Education Magazine*, 45-53.

Ediger, Marlow (2000), "The Role of the Principal in the Science Curriculum," *Experiments in Education*, 28 (2), 23-29.

Ediger, Marlow (2006), "Testing vs Portfolios to Assess Achievement," *OASCD Journal.*

National Research Council (1996), *National Science Education Standards.* Washington, DC: National Academy Press.

Supon, Viola (2006), "Using Digital Cameras for Multidimensional Learning in K-12 Classrooms, *Journal of Instructional Psychology*, 33 (2), 154-156.

Wolk, Steven (2008), "Joy in School", *Educational Leadership* 66 (1), 8-13.

Zales Charlotte Rappe, and Connie S. Unger (2008), "The Science and Literacy Framework," *Science and Children*, 46 (3), 42-45.

Oral Communication in Science Lessons and Units of Study

The four vocabularies—listening, speaking, reading and writing—interact. Growth in one area of the four interacts and makes for achievement in another. For example, a good listener should achieve more in using what has been learned involving improved speaking. Reading, as well as writing, too, provides excellent content for oral communication. The science teacher may be a positive role model in the classroom in oral communication of which vocabulary development is an important facet of experience. Reddy (2006) listed the following pertaining to vocabulary growth and development in science:

- vocabulary has an important relationship between decoding and comprehension. Vocabulary is perceived as words and meanings in the shared experience of the reader and the author. This relationship increases as reading becomes a primary tool of learning in the middle grades and the high school.
- effective teaching of vocabulary demands that it be an active process that engages students in learning new words in order to build conceptual representations of vocabulary in multiple contextual situations.
- application of remedial vocabulary instruction requires the linking of instructional strategies to the type of designed learning outcomes and student's learning capabilities.

- vocabulary knowledge supports the reader's processing of text and interacting with the author, which in turn supports the formation and validation of concepts and new learning.
- vocabulary knowledge is an indicator of student's real and vicarious experiences. Children can neither comprehend nor understand what they read unless they have some knowledge of the concepts represented in print. Knowing the meaning of words goes beyond simple definitions and getting the grist from their context. Vocabulary instruction is most effective when it is based on the association of children's experiences and concepts with the words they are learning.
- reader's conceptual and experimental backgrounds are key components in vocabulary development. Background experiences enable readers to develop and refine concepts that words represent.
- vocabulary instruction should include explicit instruction, appropriate practice and broad based opportunities for language development in a variety of texts.

Content from reading provides subject matter for oral communication activities as in discussions. A variety of rich, developmentally appropriate experiences assists in securing background information in communicating ideas orally, useful in listening, reading and writing. Oral communication has always been a major objective of instruction. The Trivium of the Middle Ages consisted of grammar, rhetoric and logic. Rhetoric (public speaking) was combined with grammar and logic to influence others in the societal arena. Cicero, the great Roman orator, placed major emphasis upon public speaking to stress the importance of convincing others to accept selected rules and regulations.

Communicating well with others orally is salient in the science curriculum Communication, here, involves a sender and one or more receivers. There are a plethora of means in communicating ideas in science such as audio recordings, video tapes, television, CD ROMS, DVDs, non-verbally, films, among others. Orally, with the spoken voice, still is a major way of communication between and among pupils and the teacher. The human voice is flexible device which is a part of the individual and does not necessarily need attending physical equipment. There are many purposes involved in the process of communicating ideas (Ediger, 2008).

Purposes in Communication in Science

Clarity is always important in oral communication since the listener needs to understand what is said. Stress is a significant concept to use in oral communication. Here, the speaker says single words louder or softer within a sentence to amplify intentions in oral communication. If the teacher says, "We will now do a *science experiment.*" The emphasis is upon doing a science experiment rather than a different kind of learning activity or in a different academic discipline. With effective use of stress in teaching and learning situations, the science teacher increases proficiency in teaching. It indicates a lack of monotony in the communication process and the presence of enthusiasm. Selected concepts and generalizations which pupils are to master might well receive adequate stress to indicate what is salient to learn. Heavy stress of spoken words shown in a sentence involve placing an exclamation mark shown at the end of a written sentence (Ediger and Rao, 2007).

A second important concept to emphasize in oral communication when teaching science is pitch. Thus, some words are pitched higher than others in context to show the following within the same sentence such as, "He did well in conducting the science experiment:"

- "He did well in conducting the science experiment?" Here, the science teacher pitches the ending words higher to have students comment on the process. It is not stated as a perceived fact. An interrogative sentence is then in evidence.
- "He did well in conducting the science experiment." Here, the teacher orally communicates a fact or opinion

with the spoken voice pitched lowest at the end. A period at the end of the written equivalent indicates a fact or opinion was communicated orally.

- "He did well in conducting the science experiment!" An exclamatory sentence shows strong feeling and has an exclamation mark at the end to show this in written work. Each word said orally has a strong stress (See National Research Council, 1996).

Thus, meanings change within the same sentence if stress is placed on different words or a word. The same is true of pauses within a sentence. Meanings change depending upon pauses within a sentence. If words in a series, for example, are stated orally, there need to be pauses of adequate length to indicate where commas would appear in writing. Misplaced modifiers, too, cause meanings to change in a sentence:

He rode to school on a bicycle with a blue scarf. "With a blue scarf," is shown as modifying the bicycle, but it rather should modify the subject of the sentence "He." With a revision, the sentence should read: "With a blue scarf, he rode to school on a bicycle." Misplaced modifiers make for possible distortions in interpretation in oral expressions (See Kieffer and Lasaux, 2007).

Reading from a developmentally appropriate basal science textbook or library book orally, involves paying careful attention to punctuation marks. A lack of understanding might well accrue due to omitting or minimizing these punctuation marks. The following lacks clarity if punctuation marks are omitted in a run on sentence: She read from the basal science textbook, wrote a summary, and used a map to show climatic changes in her oral report. To minimize these problems, fluency in oral reading also is aided with assistance in the following:

- difficulties in word recognition. The use of context clues and phonics for initial consonant sounds should help to remedy deficiencies.
- problems in reading in thought units.

- practice in oral reading of the selection, prior to its presentation in front of the class.
- peers in a group helping each other in these practice sessions (See Lockstead, 2008).

Discussions in Science

The writer when supervising university student teachers teach in the public schools has noticed specific kinds of assistance pupils need in order to communicate well in a discussion setting. The following areas need to be strengthened for pupils to communicate well:

- lack of use of complete sentences, such as omitting a subject or a predicate.
- minimizing the use of adjectives to modify nouns or adverbs to modify verbs.
- use of too few words to express content meaningfully. This may involve the need to clarify content with adjective/adverb phrases and clauses.
- rambling on with run on sentences and unnecessary wordage.
- not focusing upon the topic being discussed.
- use of irrelevant vocabulary terms and ideas (Ediger and Rao, 2007).

Discussion should consist of salient learnings which pupils receive from each other. Ideas are changed by an individual as new content is imbibed. Len S.Vygotsky (1978) was a strong advocate of pupils learning in group settings. He believed that ideas "bounce off the minds" of actively involved participants. Higher levels of cognition are then possible. Thus, pupils may discuss solutions to identified problems in an ongoing lesson/unit of study in science. A tentative hypothesis is formed which may be subject to revision within discussion settings. Critical thinking is a part of a discussion whereby facts are separated from opinions, fantasy from reality, and the relevant from the irrelevant. Also, creative thinking is needed to come up with novel, unique ideas for solutions.

Creative thinkers are important in the classroom as well as in society. Innovations and improvements come about due to creative ideas expressed in producing goods and services. Thus, science learnings may also be used to write creative poetry, to write and perform plays pertaining to leading scientists, to do drawings in art of volcanic eruptions, among others.

For young children, science picture books may be a good way to introduce and develop ideas pertaining to the natural environment. These may be used by the kindergarten and first grade teachers as well as be used in the home setting. Viewing and discussing igneous, metamorphic and sedimentary rocks first hand and then looking at their representative illustrations assist pupils to develop interest and understanding in rocks and their uses in society. One may even start with the illustrations and for example, have pupils look at and discuss simple machines. The writer has noticed in the home setting how young children like and become fascinated with simple machines in pictorial form. Many homes have concrete objects directly related to the illustrations such as a hammer to be used as a lever or a door stop used as a wedge. Also, the writer has noticed how eager young children are in viewing pictures of vertebrates and invertebrates. Vertebrates in pictorial form motivate comments, questions, and problems, even with a short attention span of very young children. Thus, fish, frogs (amphibians), turtles (reptiles), birds, and mammals capture the attention of children. These, among others, provide building blocks for sequential learning in children. Readiness for acquiring more complex facts, concepts, and generalizations are then in the offing.

Interest in science must be developed at a young age with oral communication being inherent in these ongoing learning activities. Visits to museums of natural history and/or viewing visiting displays in a community may well do much to encourage interest in science. Pupils of all ages are excited of and talk among themselves of a dinosaur exhibit. The following display of model dinosaur skeletons was recently observed locally: a brontosaurus, a dipladocus and a stegosaurs, among others. These provided ideal topics for discussion and elaboration. Many followup activities are then possible including:

- making drawings of these models.
- locating more information on dinosaurs.
- writing creative stories and poems on dinosaurs.
- pantomiming dinosaur life and having others guess which dinosaur is being pantomimed.
- doing a booklet on dinosaurs and their environment.

In Conclusion

Pupils need to have a plethora of interesting experiences in an integrated science curriculum. Listening, speaking, reading, and writing activities which accelerate quality science learnings is needed. To develop science literacy, pupils must experience rich opportunities for learning and engagement in the curriculum.

REFERENCES

Ediger, Marlow and Digumarti Bhaskara Rao (2007), *Language Arts Education*. New Delhi, India: Discovery Publishing House.

Ediger, Marlow (2008), "The School and Students in Society," *Journal of Instructional Psychology*, 35 (3), 260-263.

Ediger, Marlow and Digumarti Bhaskara Rao (2007), *School Science Education*. New Delhi, India: Discovery Publishing House (Ltd.).

Kieffer, Michael and Nancy K. Lesaux (2007), "Breaking Down Words to Build Meaning," *The Reading Teacher*, 61 (2), 146-156.

Lockstead, Larissa (2008), "Scientific Journals: A Creative Assessment Tool," *Science and Children*, 46 (3), 22-26.

National Research Council (1996), National Science Education Standards (1996). Washington, DC:, The Academy Press.

Reddy, A. M. (2006), Reading Achievement of High School Pupils in English in Relation to Certain Psycho-Sociological Variables. Tirupati, India: Sri Venkateswara University, pp. 16-17. A Ph D thesis evaluated Marlow Ediger.

Vygotsky, Len S. (1978), *Mind in Society, the Development of Higher Psychological Processes*. Cambridge, Massachusetts: Harvard University Press.

Data-driven Decision-making in Science

Data-driven decision-making is based upon more objective models of instruction than is usually the case. Thus, there is evidence available to make choices in terms of future actions in school improvement. This may be compared to using hunches, feelings, and the affective domain in decision-making. Not that feelings are all bad; there are feelings involved in any action taken in life. For example, in buying a used car, the shopper may evaluate the price of three desired automobiles and make objective comparisons here. Perhaps, they are quite uniform in quality. The buyer, though, prefers one color as compared to the others. That preference is based upon the affective domain only or largely. The buyer does not know how well each of the three cars will perform in the future. It might be the one chosen does the poorest and has the largest personal expenditures for repairs.

In pupil achievement and progress in the classroom, data driven decisions have their advantages. Thus, there is information available for choosing from among alternatives in arriving at the best decisions for assisting pupils to develop and grow (See Marice, 2005).

Decision-making in the Curriculum

The science teacher needs to be systematic in selecting those learning opportunities which guide pupil optimal progress. Thus, information might well be considered whereby numerical results tip the scales in terms of choosing pupil activities.

Mandated tests are given quite frequently in the public schools such as in grades three through eight. These are generally standardized tests. A national, reputable company has developed these tests which have been pilot tested and have accompanying norms. The pupils in the local school take these tests on their respective grade levels. The raw score an individual obtains is identified with the same score in the accompanying manual of the test which then gives the equivalent percentile or grade equivalent. The percentile given, for example, may be the 35th percentile, meaning that out of every 100 pupils taking the test, 35 are below and 65 are above that raw score received by the learner. When viewing the results on the separate test items, the science teacher makes decisions on what is needed for the pupil to achieve sequentially and more optimally. If pupils missed answers pertaining to the following concepts—igneous, sedimentary and metamorphic rocks—the science teacher needs to provide learning activities to assist pupils to understand and attach meaning to these concepts, using concrete, semi-concrete and abstract experiences for pupils. Diagnosis and remediation might well be in evidence here. Data is then used in teacher decision making (Ediger and Rao, 2007).

Teacher written tests, such as multiple choice tests, also provide data to make decisions. Each test item, generally, must have a stem with four distractors, one of which is clearly the correct answer. The stem with each distractor should be grammatically correct so that no clues are given as to which of the four is the correct answer. It is important to have all distractors of similar length so that the pupil's focus is on the possible correct answer and not to second guess as to which is correct due to its length. Teacher written tests can be strongly valid if face validity is stressed. Thus, the science teacher may write a multiple choice test item for each concept or generalization taught. Reliability may be a problem in that test results vary from one testing to the next of the same test. This would indicate test/retest reliability is emphasized. Generally or even rarely, does the teacher give the same test again to secure information on its reliability such as test/retest reliability. Standardized tests do provide reliability data in their respective manual. They are set up to do that and must, due to tests needing to measure consistently if they possess worth. For example, if a pupil received a score of fifteen correct on a fifty item test and the next time received a score of forty-five correct on the same test, the question arises as to what level is the pupil truly achieving. To run a test/retest correlation by giving the same teacher written test twice to the same pupils would waste valuable teaching time in the classroom. Or writing alternate forms of a test to check reliability is not feasible since it takes time and revisions to write these two forms of equal difficulty as well as run tests to take out weaknesses to have high quality results on reliability. For the science teacher who writes a valid multiple choice test, he/she may check reliability of that test by using split half reliability. Thus, the odd numbered are compared with the even numbered test item results, by using the Pearson Product Moment correlation. A measurement or computer specialist in the local school can run the answer sheets of pupil responses through a computer to obtain correlations. The higher the numerical results obtained for the correlation, the stronger the relationship is between the odd versus the even numbered ideas. Thus, a correlation of 80 is much superior to a correlation of 20 when comparing responses for the odd versus even numbered responses for a teacher written test. If computer services are not available to run correlations between odd versus even numbered responses, the science teacher may scan visually by noticing the consistency of responses for each pupil in the classroom to secure a rough estimate of split half reliability of test results (See National Science Teachers Association, 2001).

The science teacher needs to reflect upon pupil test results to measure science achievement. The following questions then need to be answered:

- did the test truly measure what was taught? This is a question which refers to the validity of the measurement instrument?
- were important subject matter learnings covered in the test?

- are the test items written with clarity so that misunderstandings do not occur of inherent meanings of each item to the test taker?
- were vaguely written, ambiguous test items removed or rewritten?
- according to the print out of test results, which test items did pupils answer incorrectly? Should these be retaught? Diagnosis and remediation are involved in this question.
- what do the test results imply for successful teaching?
- do the responses leave leeway for guessing? If so, lower reliability in the measurement instrument will accrue (See Brady, 2008).
- were the test data adequate to assist in making curricular decisions in science?

Data-driven decision-making depends upon using objective information to improve teaching and learning situations. Metacognitive reflection by the science teacher pertaining to test writing as well as all facets of teaching should assist in improving the curriculum. Too frequently, teachers fail to rethink what pupils experienced in science. Modification of teaching practices might well be necessary in order that each pupil achieves more optimally.

With standardized testing, the time limits for test taking are the same for all fifth graders, for example, and others of the same grade level. The directions give for test taking are the same, and the same key, of course, is use to check test scores (See Kelly, 2008).

Essay testing presents more of a problem to provide objective data, as compared to multiple choice tests. However, rubric development and use in scoring essay items tends to make the results more objective. A rubric, ideally, provides standards for scoring, generally on a five point scale for each test item to be appraised. For example in doing a science experiment on a five point scale, to receive a five—the highest rating—a pupil may be evaluated on each of the following through teacher observation:

- observes the experiment carefully without jumping to hasty conclusions.
- formulates an hypothesis based on observation.
- secures information from a variety of reference sources to check the hypothesis.
- modifies the hypothesis if necessary.
- if need be, tests the new hypothesis.

The rubric results may be used as data to improve science teaching and learning. Each of the five component parts provides feedback to the science teacher in planning ensuing lessons and units of study. Weaknesses might then be remedied.

The write up of the science experiment or other written work might well require a different rubric (Ediger, 2009). The following criteria may be developed and used to appraise written products:

- expresses ideas accurately.
- uses complete sentences in writing.
- sentences are written sequentially.
- correct spelling of words is in evidence.
- subject and predicate agree in number.

In reading science subject matter, the teacher may record the kinds of errors made by pupils and use the data to inform decision making for ensuing lessons. Thus for example in reading from the science basal, a pupil may fail to identify the word "igneous". The science teacher may list this word on a 5 × 8 inch card and provide practice for the pupil in word mastery. This should assist the learner in correctly identifying the word and knowing its contextual meaning. There are diverse kinds of specific errors pupils make in reading and these provide objectives for a future lesson:

- reading haltingly which hinders fluency in comprehension of content.
- omitting words or making substitutions for the correct word.

- not paying attention to punctuation marks such as commas, periods, question marks and exclamation points.
- failure in using proper stress, pitch and enunciation
- repeating words read correctly (Ediger, 2008).

Each of the above kinds of errors needs recording which provide feedback to the science teacher to improve comprehension in reading science content. Remedying difficulties might well help the pupil to develop an improved self concept for learning. Data-driven decisions help to objectify the selection of objectives which pupils need to achieve.

In closing

Science teachers need quality information which guide decision making in teaching and learning situations. Guesswork is then minimized in the decision making arena. Good decisions are made based on the best kind of information possible.

REFERENCES

Brady, Marion (2008), "Cover the Material—Or Teach Students to Think?" *Educational Leadership*, 65 (5), 64-67.

Ediger, Marlow (2008), "Leadership in the School Setting," *Education*, 129(1), 17-20.

Ediger, Marlow (2009), "Oral Communication in Science Teaching," *Experiments in Education*, 37 (1), 17-20.

Ediger, Marlow and Digumarti Bhaskara Rao (2007), *School Science Education*. New Delhi, India: Discovery Publishing House.

Kelly, William E. (2008), "Psychometric Properties and Correlates of the Robert Morris Attention Scale," *Reading Improvement*, 45 (1),19-25.

Marice, F. W. (2005), Problem Solving Ability, Aptitude, Attitude, and Competency in Teaching Science Trainees in Colleges of Education in Kerala. Ph D Thesis University of Madras, India, evaluated by Marlow Ediger.

National Science Teacher Association (2001), *Classroom Assessment and the National Education Standards*. Washington, DC: NSTA.

16 Readiness for Learning in Science

Readiness is an important factor in learning. This is true of any lesson and unit of study in science. The science teacher must make decisions pertaining to prerequisites which have/have not been mastered prior to stressing pupils achieving a new objective. If pupils are not ready for the ensuing learnings, they will experience frustration. New objectives must be challenging and yet be achievable by the learner. Enjoyment and excitement in learning are salient in science to make for more optimal progress.

The science teacher must be well-prepared for each day of teaching so that pupils might attain relevant objectives, experience stimulating learning activities, as well as quality evaluation techniques which provide feedback to the teacher as well as pupils to improve the curriculum (Ediger and Rao, 2007).

Readiness and the Learner

How is readiness secured within pupils? One salient factor is to have learners possess adequate background information in order to benefit from ensuing experiences. Thus, in order to benefit from a unit on magnetism and electricity, pupils need selected understandings. The teacher, depending upon the maturation level of involved pupils, may have different materials in paper cups such as bits of paper, wood, steel nails, marbles, and cereal. Pupils individually might then hypothesize which items from the separate cups will be attracted by a bar or horse shoe magnet. Responses need to be recorded.

Additional readiness may be emphasized such as testing a suspended bar magnet from string with another magnet to determine if like poles attract or repel. Most pupils enjoy these activities. They also like to experiment with magnets on their own. These experiences, among others, provide readiness for pupils to benefit more fully from the new unit on magnetism and electricity. With needed prerequisite learnings, pupils are better able to achieve challenging objectives of instruction. The readiness experiences need to harmonize sequentially with the new learnings to be acquired. A seamless science curriculum is an end result (See Gilbert and Kotelman, 2005).

In addition to having met readiness prerequisites, pupils also must perceive purpose in and for an ensuing unit of study. Purpose for learning resides within the pupil, not within the teacher. The latter assists in setting the stage for pupils perceiving purpose or reasons for learning. Reasons for attaining objectives then are in evidence. To perceive purpose, the pupil needs to become engaged in ongoing learning activities and intrinsically accept reasons for active participation. The teacher may briefly explain a purpose for the ensuing lesson, for example, by stating why pupils need to experience a unit on electricity and magnetism. This may be done, for example, by indicating how magnets pick up heavy loads of metal to be loaded onto a truck. The principle here of opposite poles attract is being emphasized such as a north pole attracting a south pole. If a teacher stated purpose does not motivate, then having pupils hypothesize reasons for learning about magnets might well be stressed. Generally, pupils come up with one or more reasons (See National Research Council, 1996).

Third, pupils must experience interest in learning as a readiness factor. Interest propels pupil achieving of objectives of instruction. The learning opportunity and the learner become one and not separated from each other. If separation of the two occur, then perhaps little learning takes place.

Hopefully, the pupil will become interested to the point that wholehearted involvement is in evidence. There are times when a pupil may desire to have the time extended for learning and achievement in science. Interest is a vital criterion to stress in science learning. When supervising university student teachers in the public schools, the writer has noticed primary grade pupils huddled around an aquarium discussing the observed fish swimming. They discussed and raised many questions such as how gills operate for fish to survive underwater. The natural environment provides a plethora of interest centers for pupils. Outside of the school setting, pupils notice interesting phenomenon such as why a mud puddle dried up, after a rain. Here, the pupil may learn about the water cycle such as moisture in the form of rain followed by needed factors for evaporation. Also, pupils may bring science objects to school for show and tell experiences which, for example, might well include tadpoles in a jar from a farm pond. These tadpoles will then be observed to notice the growth of feet and eventually become a mature frog. Excitement is in the air with pupil eagerness to tell about their show and tell objects (See Blough and Schwartz, 1984).

Fourth, a quality current events program in science might well provide readiness for learning. In any newscast or news paper for children, there are a plethora of incidences which have just occurred. Thus, news items such as the following have occurred in different areas of the world:

- earthquakes, tornados, hurricanes.
- mudslides, volcanic eruptions, gully and sheet erosion.
- ice storms, floods, drought, hail and strong wind gusts.

Each of the above provide content for elaboration and discussions. Audio-visual aids provide for clarity in current events presentations. Problem-solving activities may occur through identifying a problem pertaining to the causes of each of the above, developing an hypothesis, evaluating the hypothesis and making necessary modifications and revisions. Indepth learnings may then occur.

At the beginning of the primary school years, pupils already may develop conclusions in problem-solving based on their individual maturity levels. All science teaching includes the following considerations:

- are the learnings on the understanding level of individual pupils?
- might pupils be motivated to realize high expectations?
- will the content be sequenced appropriately for optimal pupil progress?
- may indepth learning follow the readiness experiences? (See Maheshwari, 2008).

Fifth, pupils need assistance to scaffold information. If, for example, a pupil did not attach meaning to the concept "reptiles", the science teacher may scaffold sequential activities to aid in its understanding. Depending upon the maturity level of the learner, the teacher might show pictures in the basal science textbook of snakes and turtles and briefly/clearly state why these are reptiles. The learner may verbalize, in return, what a reptile is to provide feedback to the teacher in revealing its understanding. With scaffolding, the pupil is able to learn more complicated subject matter than otherwise would be the case. Subject matter chosen for scaffolding must be achievable, not beyond the capability of the pupil. The science teacher needs to receive feedback from the learner to notice if efforts at scaffolding have worked. If not, additional strategies need to be in the offing (Vygotsky, 1933, 1978).

Sixth, metacognition must be stressed. Here, the pupil reflects upon what has/has not been learned. Thus, a pupil thinks about previous learnings to notice if readiness exists to acquire the ensuing subject matter. The science teacher, also, must reflect upon previously used teaching strategies to notice what worked and what did not work effectively. Modifications in teaching might then be made such as in the following:

- from the use of abstract learnings to emphasizing concrete experiences for pupils.

- from rote learning to problem solving activities.
- from lecture to inquiry learning.
- from reading about science to doing science as in performing experiments, the heart of the science curriculum.
- from being passive recipients of knowledge to actively pursuing tasks as in the project method.
- from memorizing science subject matter to engaging in problem-solving.

Seventh, learning styles (Searson and Dunn, 2001) have salient implications for teaching and learning. To provide readiness for learning, each pupil prefers a particular style more so than others. Thus, selected pupils may prefer cooperative learning rather than experiencing individual activities. The former have preferences to learn within a committee setting as compared to the latter who prefer to engage in learning opportunities by the self. For example in using the project method, a set of learners select to work together in developing a model volcano in an ongoing unit of study, whereas another pupil chooses to work on a model pertaining to folding and faulting individually. Further differences in styles of learning include the following:

- teacher guided instruction as compared to an open ended science curriculum.
- a subject-centered science curriculum instead of using pupil-centered procedures.
- the use of behaviorally stated objectives in instruction versus open ended objectives in teaching and learning situations.
- a separate subjects science curriculum versus integrated units of study relating many academic disciplines.

The science teacher then must take into consideration under which conditions pupils learn best in ongoing lessons and units of study. Optimal pupil achievement is desired and therefore learning styles need consideration in choosing learning opportunities. Readiness for learning requires that science teachers take into consideration how pupils learn.

Eighth, readiness for learning must also take into consideration multiple intelligences theory. Thus, a pupil may possess one or more intelligences in the acquisition of knowledge and skills. Science has its own methods and subject matter. However, related content from other disciplines might assist pupils to achieve more optimally. The following intelligences may be brought in as needed to clarify and extend subject matter learnings:

- verbal as in reading and writing experiences.
- logical as in reasoning about science phenomenon.
- musical as in writing lyrics and putting them to music.
- intrapersonal as in showing much strengths in working by the self.
- interpersonal as in revealing much achievement in cooperative learning.
- bodily/kinesthetic as in doing high quality projects and construction work.
- scientific in thinking objectively in learnings dealing with the natural and social environment (See Gardner, 1993).

Ninth, portfolios might well assist the science teacher in determining pupil readiness for learning. Traditional or digital portfolios contain a representative sampling of pupil work in science lessons and units of study such as the following:

- book reports on science content.
- photos of science projects and construction work, individually and/or committee endeavors.
- samples of oral reading activities.
- results from teacher written and standardized tests.
- self-evaluation in terms of recommended criteria.
- art work products completed in science lessons and units of study.
- creative written work as in writing poems and stories.

By examining each of the above, the science teacher is better able to ascertain pupil readiness for learning as well as to assess pupil progress (Ediger, 2008-2009).

Tenth, a variety of evaluation procedures need to be used to ascertain learner achievement in science. These procedures must be valid and reliable, using the best criteria in the evaluation process when using:

- teacher written tests.
- standardized and mandated tests.
- teacher observation.
- product and process evaluation.

REFERENCES

Blough, Glenn O. and Julius Schwartz (1984), *Elementary School Science and How To Teach It*. New York: Holt, Rinehart and Winston.

Ediger, Marlow and Digumarti Bhaskara Rao (2007), *School Science Education*. New Delhi, India: Discovery Publishing House (Ltd.).

Ediger, Marlow (2008-2009) "Portfolios in Science," *Connecticut Journal of Science Education*, 47 (1), 28-29.

Gilbert, Jean and Marleen Kotelman (2005), Five Good Reasons to use Science Notebooks," *Science and Children*, 43 (3), 28-32.

Gardner, Howard (1993), *Multiple Intelligences: Theory Into Practice*. New York: Basic Books.

Maheshwari, Amrita (2008), "Integral Values of Science Education," *Edutracks*, 8 (4), 16-17.

National Research Council (1996), *National Science Education Standards*. Washington, DC: National Academy Press.

Searson, Robert and Rita Dunn (2001), "The Learning Styles Teaching Model," *Science and Children*, 38 (5), 22-36.

Vygotsky, L. S. (1933, 1978), *Mind in Society: The Development of Higher Psychological Processes*. Cambridge, Massachusetts: Harvard University Press.

The Psychology of Learning and the Science Curriculum

The psychology of learning is important to emphasize in teaching science since pupil achievement is then optimized. There are selected standards then which are stressed in teaching and learning situations. Interest, as one factor, is salient to stress so that pupils are on task in going lessons and learning opportunities (See Gilbert and Kotelman, 2005). Which standards from the psychology of learning should then be inherent in teaching science?

Learning Opportunities to Achieve Objectives

To achieve relevant, salient objectives in science, pupils need to experience quality instruction. Quality in instruction emphasizes teacher use of education psychology to assist pupil progress. Thus, meaning theory should be stressed continuously as pupils acquire vital science facts, concepts and generalizations. Pupil need to be able to explain what has been achieved. Merely memorizing or parroting back what the science teacher has explained does not stress learning. Rather, the pupil should be able to explain in his/her own words what the acquired content means. Thus, the learner is in a better position to build upon previous learnings when participating in an ensuing experience. A connection needs to exist between the old and new ideas gleaned. Further relationships must be formed between the pupil and his/her personal experiences. Thus, the science curriculum needs to be related to functional experiences of the learner. What has been learned or is being learned must be useful in school and in society. Science needs to be connected, also, to other branches of knowledge such as mathematics which is the language of science (Ediger and Rao, 2007).

Behaviorism, as a school of psychology, emphasizes that precise, measurably stated objectives need to be determined for classroom teaching. The science teacher must emphasize relevant, precise objectives, written, for pupils to achieve. The degree of precision generally will make it so that pupils either do/do not achieve the objective. Measurability is salient here. E. L. Thorndike (1874-1949) believed that whatever exists, exists in some amount and if it exists, it can be measured. Tests are then developed to measure what is stated in the objective. Standardized tests fit this pattern to measure what exists. Here, pupils on a certain grade level take the same test, within the same allotted time, using the same directions in taking the test. Validity and reliability data are provided in the standardized test's manual which makes it possible to compare one's own pupil's results with those in the norm group. The norm group who took the test and their results provided data on what one's own pupils would rank percentile wise. If, for example, a pupil in the science teacher's classroom received a raw score of 60 on the standardized science test, this would equal the 75th percentile, as shown in the Manual (See Marice, 2005).

Much effort and expense go into the development of a standardized test. The science teacher may write his/her own test based upon the objectives emphasized in class. He/she is also teaching toward ends or objectives which pupils are to achieve. Diagnosis is involved if the science teacher analyzes data from these tests to notice what needs reteaching. There are a plethora of reasons for a pupil not having secured a correct answer such as:

- not having understood what was being taught.
- sequence in learning was not in evidence.

- not having paid attention to ongoing learning experiences.
- not being on task.
- not participating actively in an ongoing lesson (See Condrey, 1996).

The science teacher may also appraise his/her own teaching by looking back at what might have caused learners to make these errors. A different teaching strategy may need to be implemented in order to guide optimal learner achievement.

Behaviorism then stresses the use of precise objectives in teaching where there is agreement among educators as to what pupils are to learn within each stated objective. Tests must be aligned with the stated objectives. Valid and reliable tests then should convey what pupils have learned as a result of testing.

Somewhat opposite of behaviorism is humanism as a psychology of education. A. H. Maslow's (1954) hierarchy of needs is salient to stress here. Maslow indicated five levels of meeting pupil needs in the total development of the individual. These are:

- meeting the physiological needs of pupils such as adequate food, clothing and shelter.
- taking care of safety needs of pupils including physical and mental safety such as freedom from harassment, emotional and social abuse.
- belonging needs in that pupils desire to belong to and be accepted within groups. Rejection is a negative feeling.
- esteem needs. Here, the pupil wishes to receive recognition for accomplishment and achievement. Being ignored or ridiculed does not meet the esteem needs criteria.
- becoming the kind of person desired.

The individual is viewed holistically when studying the above-named criteria.

Humanism emphasizes decision-making and choices in terms of what to learn and this is stressed within a framework. There are several plans available to stress humanism in the science curriculum. One plan is the contract agreed upon by the pupils with teacher assistance. Here, the pupil decides upon what he/she wishes to complete within a designated time, which may be modified if need be. Thus from an ongoing science unit of study, the pupil, for example, agrees to complete the following:

- do three activities from the enrichment center.
- read a library book and summarize its findings.
- view a video tape and develop a related model.
- do four science experiments and draw relevant conclusions.

The contract is signed by the pupils and by the teacher with the due date provided. All completed work is to show effort and neatness. The plan is developed by the involved learner and has teacher supervision. Evaluation of the products involve both pupil and teacher.

Carl Rogers (1983) was a leading advocate of using humanism as a psychology of learning. As a young boy, he had a unique interest in moths. Fortunately, his primary grade teacher shared and encourage this personal interest. Rogers believed children were naturally curious about their environment and extended and developed interests in depth. Pupils should then try out their very own ideas without fear of ridicule or facing rude comments. Self directed learning and choosing what to learn are salient. Being a motivated pupil increases as he/she select what to pursue. Implications here for the science teacher are the following:

- assist pupils to choose their own purposes in learning.
- guide pupils to become responsible learners.
- promote life-long learning by having pupils select what is interesting to learn and engages each learner.

Humanism then focuses upon the individual pupil in the teaching and learning process. Small group and committee learning are to be emphasized if based on learner interests. Vygotsky (1933,1978) stressed the importance of cooperative learning whereby pupils interact with each other in ideas expressed and growth in achievement comes about in a social situation. Ideas then "bounce off the minds of pupils" as they pursue a concept or generalization.

Constructivism in the Science Curriculum

Constructivism, as a psychology of learning, is also pupil centered. Pupils then are actively involved in selecting, with teacher assistance, what to learn in ongoing units of study. Sequence resides within the pupil, not the teacher. The learner sequences what comes next in pursuing an activity or a project. The learner makes connections between preceding experiences and the ensuing science lesson/unit of study. Questions from pupils are encouraged so that gaps in learning may be minimized. These gaps are perceived when a pupil does not perceive closure between the known and the unknown in ensuing science subject matter being studied. Questions are also asked when curiosity is inherent in wondering about specifics in the natural environment, such as having seen dew on grass in the morning on a nice spring day, adjacent to the school. The learner then wants to know why dew occurs. This may expand to performing science experiments to show causes of dew in the natural environment. Curiosity of pupils must be motivated so that pupils develop attitudes necessary for achieving objectives in the science curriculum (See National Research Council, 1996).

Problem identification by pupils is salient for a constructivist emphasis in teaching and learning situations. John Dewey (1916) was an early advocate of using problem solving methods of teaching. Within a science unit, pupils select a problem area which requires deliberation, critical and creative thinking. An hypothesis is developed in response to the problem. The hypothesis needs testing with the use of experimentation, the internet, science encyclopedias, among others, as information sources. The hypothesis is then refuted, modified, or accepted as is.

Within a problem solving activity, pupils with teacher guidance, are actively involved in identification of the problem, developing an hypothesis, as well as choosing a variety of reference sources to use in its evaluation. These processes are ordered and sequenced by involved learners.

Project methods are also pupil centered. This method was developed by William Heard Kilpatrick (1918). He emphasized pupil purposing, pupil planning, pupils caring out the plan, and pupil evaluation of the product. The project method is very salient presently as a method of teaching whereby the learner is heavily involved in the total process. Thus the pupil, for example, individually or collectively determine a project such as developing models of as well as a chart showing classifications of vertebrates and invertebrates. Both need carefully planning in order to complete quality products. Adherence to a well developed plan makes for meticulous work among involved learners. Approved criteria are developed and used to appraise the final product. Here, pupils, too, sequence their very own work, as is typical of constructivism as a psychology of learning.

In Conclusion

Tenets from the psychology of learning need to be studied and implemented to assist pupils to achieve more optimally. Pupils possess different styles of learning. The following are preferences which pupils have pertaining to their individual method of processing information and skills:

- a structured science curriculum as compared to one being more open ended.
- teacher selection of learning opportunities for pupils as compared to learners largely sequencing their own experiences.
- teachers appraising learner achievement, or pupils being heavily involved in the assessment process.

REFERENCES

Condrey, Jean Friend (1996), "Focus on Science Concepts," *The Science Teacher*, 63 (4), 23-28.

Dewey, John (1916), *Democracy and Education*. New York: Macmillan Company.

Ediger, Marlow and Digumarti Bhaskara Rao (2007), *School Science Education*. New Delhi, India: Discovery Publishing House.

Gilbert, Joan, and Marleen Kottelman (2007), "Five Good Reasons to Use Science Notebooks," *Science and Children*, 43 (3), 28-32.

Kilpatrick, William Heard (1918), *The Project Method*. New York: Teacher's College, Columbia University.

Marice, P. V. (2005), Problem Solving Ability, Aptitude and Competency in Science Trainees In Colleges of Education in Kerala. Ph D thesis evaluated by Marlow Eiger for University of Madras, Chennai, India.

Maslow, A. H. (1954) *Motivation and Personality*. New York: Harper and Row

National Research Council (1996). National Science Education Standards. Washington DC: National Academy Press.

Rogers, Carl (1983), *Freedom to Learn: A View of What Education Might Become*. Columbus, Ohio: Charles Merrill Company.

Vygotsky, Len S. (1933-1978), *Mind in Society: The Development of Higher Psychological Processes*. Cambridge, Massachusetts: Harvard University Press.

Methods of Teaching Science

There are a Plethora of methods to use in teaching science. The science teacher needs to study and assess diverse approaches in teaching and learning situations. Innovative procedures may be tried out and if found suitable, integrated into the science curriculum. Individual differences among students in the classroom need adequate provision. The needs of each student must be met. This requires the teacher to use diverse methods of teaching since students differ from each other in style(s) of learning, in science knowledge and in intelligence(s) possessed (Ediger and Rao, 2007).

The Student and the Teaching of Science

Technology use in schools continues to increase at a rapid rate. Computer Assisted Instruction (CAI) and its implementation has made teaching students as interacting with a program in a computer. The science program used must relate directly to the unit of study being taught as well as being on the developmental level of the learner. Additional considerations include:

- evaluating the present status of the learner's achievement with a pre-test.
- providing science subject manner in a meaningful manner.
- presenting drill and practice activities to fix knowledge in the mind of the learner.

- assisting pupil interest in learning with a gaming approach.
- assessing pupil knowledge by using a post-test.
- walking learners through a sequence of soft ware teaching packages.
- keeping a record of test scores to notice achievement (See Wiske, 2004).

The level of subject matter difficulty in science needs to be appropriate for student acquisition in CAI programs. Science vocabulary terms used in each program must assist students to attach meaning to ongoing experiences. Accuracy of subject matter is inherent and does not contain offensive stereotype materials offensive to anyone. The purpose for interacting with CAI materials should be clear to the student. Quality sequence in learnings is important so that successful achievers are in evidence. Graphics, color and sound, should promote the learning of science. Each program should assist students to learn, grow and develop. Feedback to learners' responses provides necessary and valuable information for the ensuing items to be learned (Djeassilane, 2008).

Virtual reality is stressed in computerized instruction. Thus, experimentation, being at the heart of the science curriculum, is shown as meaningfully as possible. The following then becomes a part of virtual reality in using computer aided instruction:

- showing which objects such as wood, glass, or metals, are/are not attracted by magnets.
- showing that air has weight and takes up space.
- showing the affects of gravity using toy cars and an inclined plane.
- showing the use of simple machines in performing work.
- showing how work is calculated in using foot pounds.

Processes, also, may readily be shown on the monitor portraying complete metamorphoses of an insect such as an egg, larva, pupa and adult, as in a butterfly (See Zahra, 2008).

CAI might well be compared with a more traditional, but recommended approach in teaching science. In an ongoing science unit, the teacher may show or involve pupils in doing an experiment, for example, on what plants need in order to grow. Two potted plants of similar stock may be shown to learners. The same amount of recommended fertilizer, water, and sunlight, among other necessary factors need to be kept constant initially. One variable needs to be tested in terms of plant needs such as placing a box over one of the two plants to observe what happens. In a period of time, pupils might well notice the affects of a plant not receiving sunlight. After the plant recovers, the next variable to control is omission of water for one of the two plants. This may be followed with testing additional variables in terms of what a plant needs to grow well. For each experiment, pupils:

- must possess adequate background information in order to understand each concept in the experiment.
- need to perceive the purpose of each experiment.
- should be actively involved in achieving.
- must attach meaning to ongoing experiences (Ediger, 2008).

Inquiry learning works well with quality ongoing experiments. Curious pupils may hypothesize as to what will transpire in the experiment. They may then check the outcomes of their hypotheses through careful observation of the experiment. Good discussions, using proper criteria, will assist in involving all students in the activity. Critical and creative thinking as well as problem solving encourage pupils to engage in higher cognitive levels of thinking. Indepth learning might well then be in evidence. Additional extended learnings include reading about related concepts from the internet, the basal textbook and/or science encyclopedias. Pupils may also:

- write up a science experiment.
- participate in small group discussions.
- do a related project, based upon science subject matter being studied.

- develop and present an oral report on a selected facet of the ongoing science unit.
- make a model individually or within a committee setting (See National Research Council, 1996).

A variety of learning activities need to be provided to assist each pupil to select an activity to complete. The activity is challenging and yet achievable. *Scaffolding* is a valuable concept for the teacher to use in teaching and learning situations. Thus, if a pupil does not understand a generalization in science, the teacher may use a series of small steps sequentially in teaching to help the pupil achieve the original complex idea. Pupils, also, need to develop a monitoring approach of their ongoing learnings to notice if meaning is being attached. If meaning is lacking, the pupil must be aided to ask questions so that the unknown becomes knowable subject matter (See Cuniff and McMillen, 1996).

Metacognition emphasizes that pupils "think about thinking." Thus in a problem solving activity in science, the pupil needs to think about the sequential steps used in coming up with a tentative solution. The learner then reflects upon involved processes used. Then too, in learning about vocabulary terms in an ongoing science unit of study, the pupil thinks about how these were learned and reflects upon the meanings attached. It is necessary to do this so that learnings are retained and used. In supervising university student teachers in the public schools, the cooperating teacher modelled the concept of metacognition aloud for pupils with the following vocabulary terms studied in context a few days/weeks previously:

- properties of matter.
- position and motion of objects.
- light, heat and magnetism.

The above-named physical science terms were then reviewed and rehearsed by pupils as an advantage in seeing a model of the application of metacognition. Learners need to use what has been achieved or it will become hazy or forgotten.

In Closing

Two methods were discussed in teaching science. CAI is highly structured which follows a programmed learning model. The pupil here interacts with a computer and software. Relevant learnings may be obtained with an interesting program, carefully sequenced.

The second method discussed emphasized a multi-media approach with pupil/teacher interaction. A variety of media were used in teaching and learning situations. Teachers need to become highly knowledgeable of each procedure and stress what meets individual needs of pupils in science (See Horesji, 2003).

REFERENCES

Cuniff, Patricia A. and Janet K. Me Millen (1996), "Field Studies," *The Science Teacher*, 63 (51) 55-60.

Djeassilane, N. (2008), Computer Aided Instruction (CAI) in Enhancing the Academic Achievement of Higher Secondary Students in Commerce. Ph D thesis evaluated by the Marlow Ediger for Alagappa University, Karaikudi-630 003, India.

Ediger, Marlow (2008), "Leadership in the School Setting," *Education*, 129 (1), 17-20.

Ediger, Marlow and Digumarti Bhaskara Rao (2007), *Science Curriculum and Instruction*. New Delhi, India: Discovery Publishing House (Ltd.).

Horesji, Martin (2003), "Making Technology Inclusive," *Science and Children*, 41 (3), 20-24.

National Research Council (1996), *National Science Education Standards*. Washington, DC: National Academy Press.

Wiske, S. (2004), "Use Technology to dig for Meaning," *Educational Leadership*, 63(1).

Zahra, Anne (2008), "Limitless Images: Digital Photography in the classroom," *The Delta Kappa Gamma Bulletin*, 75 (1), 7-9, 17.

Portfolios in Science

There are a plethora of methods which may be used to appraise pupil achievement in science. Portfolios are a significant approach. They may contain a representative sampling of actual pupil work in science. Teacher guidance is needed in developing the pupil portfolio. Pupils may use the portfolio to review what has been learned. Parents may also perceive what their offspring has learned in science units of study by looking at and asking questions about pupil performance. Among other times, this may occur at parent/teacher conferences. Here questions might be asked and answers clarified about a child's performance in science (Ediger, 2006).

Philosophy of Portfolio Use

Portfolios emphasize constructivism as a philosophy of instruction and evaluation. What is salient to learn is not measurable in many situations including motivation and attitudes within a specific science unit of study. The whole child is involved in learning such as the intellectual, the physical, the attitudinal, as well as the social dimension. More than specific parts of the learner are inherent in that various areas of growth and development are involved in achievement. Constructivism stresses open-ended objectives which provide flexible means of teaching and leave considerable leeway for pupil input. Thus, pupils have more control of their very own learning than is true of many classrooms. Evaluation tends to be more subjective as compared to using measurement procedures to assess pupil progress. Self-evaluation by the pupil with teacher guidance is also emphasized (Ediger and Rao, 2007).

Constructivism stresses that pupils largely develop their own understandings with the assistance of the teacher. Motivational learning activities then need to be in the offing. Problem solving experiences in context are encouraged. Pupil curiosity in ongoing science units encourages learners to ask questions and identify problem areas. A variety of reference sources are used to secure information whereby an hypothesis is developed and tested. Science experiments and demonstrations need to be incorporated as sources of information as well as being the heart of problem solving activities. The internet also provides valuable information as well as the more traditional procedures such as science textbook use, science encyclopedias, library books and resource people who specialize in the knowledge being sought by pupils (See National Research Council, 1996).

To constructionists, knowledge is not learned for its own sake, but it is to be used in functional situations such as to solve problems as well as to engage in project methods of achievement. It is not learned separate from skills since knowledge is to be applied. The level of application is very salient and it does eliminate/minimize what the student perceives as having little value or worth. Knowledge, too, is viewed as wholistic, rather than as separate subjects/components or categories to be mastered. A well balanced curriculum of subject matter (science, mathematics, social studies, and the language arts), as well as the fine/practical arts, and health and physical education are to be experienced by learners. Then too, personality development is salient including quality ethics, caring for others, assisting people, and as well as good attitudes in general (See Beckstead, 2008).

Constructivism then stresses students developing a portfolio of randomized products showing what has been learned within a given period of time. The following may then become a vital part of a student's portfolio:

- a comprehensive write up of science experiments and demonstrations.
- electronic photos of art work, murals, models and committee work participated in ongoing science units of study.
- essays, poems, summaries, and book reports written as a part of different science lessons/units of study.
- recordings of oral book reports and summaries of concluded science learnings (See Rose, 1999).

Testing to Notice Student Progress in Science

As compared to constructivism, testing stresses measurability of learner achievement. Thus, it can be measured to show quantitatively learner progress in diverse academic disciplines, including science. With quantitative data, students may be compared against each other in terms of achievement. The comparisons then reveal percentile differences among learners. A student may be on the 75th percentile, meaning out of every 100 students tested, 75 were below the 75th percentile. Or if a student was on the fiftieth percentile, out of every 100 tested, fifty students were above and fifty below the fiftieth percentile. E.L. Thorndike (1874-1949) stated basic beliefs pertaining to the measurement movement, "Anything that exists, exists in some amount, and if it exists in some amount, it can be measured." Questions arise pertaining to the following being measurable:

- caring for and assisting others as needed.
- humanitarian feelings (See Wolk, 2008).

Standardized tests for attitudes, for example, toward science or other academic disciplines have a rather low rating for reliability, This means that these kinds of tests do not measure in a reliable manner. Thus, a student may take a test over again and the results may differ considerably from the first to the second time of testing. A highly reliable test has high correlations between alternate forms of a test, split half reliability, or test/retest reliability.

Standardized tests developed by a commercial company and, generally, for a specific age or grade level:

- contain clear directions for test taking.
- specific time limits for test taking.
- the same key used for computerized scoring of all tests.
- mass numbers of tests scored with modern technology.

Testing is to be objective and free from opinions and biases. The only variable in testing situations is the individual student and his/her knowledge of subject matter. All other conditions are kept constant. In the case of mandated objectives, additional criteria for standardized tests include the following:

- pilot studies having been run to ascertain validity and reliability.
- student results given in quantitative terms such as percentiles and/or grade equivalents.
- norms provided to indicate where one's own students are achieving in relationship to those quantified from the pilot studies (Ediger, 2008).

Conclusion

Regardless of the teaching philosophy emphasized, the science teacher needs to provide pupils with interesting goal centered experiences. He/she also needs to:

- assist learners to be actively engaged in learning.
- help pupils perceive meaning in learning.
- motivate pupils to achieve, grow, and develop, in ongoing science units of study.
- guide learners to experience purpose in learning.

REFERENCES

Beckstead, Larissa (2008), "Scientific Journals: A Creative Assessment Tool," *Science and Children*, 46 (3), 22-26.

Ediger, Marlow (2006), "Testing Versus Portfolios to Assess Achievement," *OASCD Journal*, 13 (1), 31-32.

Ediger, Marlow (2008), "Leadership in the School Setting," *Education*, 129 (1), 17-20.

Ediger, Marlow and Digumarti Bhaskara Rao (2007), *School Science Education*. New Delhi, India: Discovery Publishing House.

National Research Council (1996), *National Science Education Standards*. Washington, DC: National Academy Press.

Rose, M. (1999), *Ten Easy Writing Lessons That Get Kids Ready for Writing Assessments*. New York: Scholastic.

Wolk, Steven (2008), "Joy in School," *Educational Leadership*, 66 (1), 8-14.

20 Mentoring and the Science Teacher

The mentor is one who is highly knowledgeable about science content as well as methods of teaching. He/she is able to work effectively and well with others. The mentor is able to motivate science teachers to teach students to achieve more optimally, using a variety of recommended approaches.

Mentoring is a procedure which, among others, helps teachers in inservice education and to update teaching methods in science. Quality science teaching needs to be emphasized and continuous growth is necessary.

Science teachers need to develop a philosophy of instruction which which provides direction in teaching and learning. There are theories of learning which provide guidance involving the teacher in making curricular decisions. Science teachers need to model that which is objective and truly independent of any observer. Objectivity, among other facets, then is a key element to stress in teaching science. Teachers with a rich, solid base of science content have more to offer than isolated facts. The base is useful in guiding students to develop functional concepts, generalizations, main ideas and applicable skills (Ediger and Rao, 2007).

The Science Teacher in the Mentoring Process

Mentors need to possess a nourishing and professional relationship with science teachers. He/she needs to possess the knowledge, skills and attitudes to assist science teachers in continual growth and achievement in the teaching/learning processes. What roles do mentors play in efforts at curriculum improvement?

The methods of science need much emphasis in the curriculum. Careful observation, inquiry methods and problem solving are major goals to stress. Individuals live in a world of science with rapid inventions in the area of technology. Scientists have provided the latest technology to improve the human condition. Labor saving devices have made the world of work easier and more efficient. Medical science has provided better health practices and care among humans. Many deadly diseases of the past are no longer a major threat such as polio, diphtheria and cholera. With a longer life span, individuals experience an increase in cancer, heart attacks, strokes, and diabetes. New threats in bacterial and viral mutations do make for ensuing threats to human health. In addition to labor saving devices, as well as better health care and life expectancy, Agricultural and food supplies have increased in productivity. Supermarkets abound in food products and for many people, obesity is a problem. The writer taught on the West Bank of the Jordan for two years and observed bedouins (nomads) frequently. Bedouins are very slender, living in harsh conditions in a desert setting with food being in extremely short supply. There are no problems with obesity in bedouin life observed (Ediger, 2007).

The objectives for student attainment need to be clarified so that definite goals are to be achieved by learners. They need to be set at a level which are developmentally appropriate for students. Objectives which are too difficult may well lead to frustration or student failure. Toward the other extreme, Relatively easy objectives to attain might lead to boredom. With clarified objectives, it is necessary to align learning activities with these chosen ends of instruction.

The learning activities need to engage learners in ongoing lessons and units of study. These include individual and small group experiences such as the following:

- reading from the science basal text, library books, science encyclopedias, as well as needed information from the internet.
- emphasizing project methods which relate to the ongoing science lesson/unit of study.
- engaging in problem solving experiences which involve a problem, an hypothesis and a tentative conclusion, subject to further testing.
- taking excursions, as well as doing journal writing, diary entries, and note taking.
- making models pertaining to concepts and generalizations studied in science (See National Research Council, 1996).

Performing science experiments is the heart of the science curriculum. Throughout each of the above asterisked items, a related experiment may be conducted. If possible, safe and developmentally appropriate, students should be involved in doing the experiment. Carefully planned and initiated, each experiment should be clearly visible to learners. There must be a purpose for each science experiment and that being to make a concept/generalization meaningful to students. It is a vital approach in teaching and is central to science learnings. Student interest in science may certainly be stimulated with quality experiments. Processes used in science should assist students to make valid predictions, accurate observations, make good inferences, classify information, as well as communicate effectively. Students should also learn to ask quality questions, visualize subject matter, and summarize information obtained. It is salient for learners to make connections with the science subject matter acquired by making use of what has been learned. Relating content presently learned to subject matter previously acquired assists in integrating and retaining ideas (See Fitzhugh, 2006).

Higher Levels of Cognition

Mentors need to help science teachers guide students to do more intensive thinking. This means that indepth learning will be fostered regardless of the learning activity pursued in ongoing lessons and science units of study. Analytic thinking is highly useful to emphasize. Here, the student is guided to separate facts from opinions, accurate from inaccurate statements, as well as fantasy from reality. Objective thinking is then being stressed. A synthesis of thought should occur after analyzing content being studied. Problem solving, for example, emphasizes that students synthesized information in order to secure an hypothesis or tentative answer. Also, project methods stress the importance of integrating science subject matter in order to engage in making models and doing construction work.

Science teachers need to assist students to reflect upon what has been learned. Thus after reading science subject matter, the student mentally rethinks what has been read and might well answer the following questions:

- which major ideas did I comprehend?
- how did the related illustrations assist in understanding what was read?
- in the large and small group discussions, which ideas were clarified from my reading of information?
- how did the internet help to secure additional information?
- what would I like to learn which was not covered in the above-named questions (Ediger, 2007)?

The science teacher must learn to use metacognition strategies in teaching and learning situations. Thus, he/she rehearses what was taught with the intent of improving over previous times. The teacher views what might have been changed to:

- secure more wholehearted involvement of learners in the ongoing lesson in science.
- develop student learnings more indepth pertaining to specific identified concepts.
- improve student sequence in learning.
- assist learners to understand identified vital vocabulary terms.

Evaluation of Achievement

Mentors have much responsibility in assisting science teachers in appraising student achievement. The appraisal results should provide feedback to the teacher in assisting learner achievement. Teacher observation of students is one significant procedure. Here, the teacher must use proper criteria in the evaluation process. These criteria may be inherent in the following by assessing:

- portfolios developed by pupils of representative work in ongoing science units of study.
- on task behavior in ongoing science lessons.
- student responsibility for completing and doing well in assigned activities.
- learners being meticulous in processes involving the project method.
- active participation of students in small and large discussion groups.
- scientific journals kept of investigations and experiments conducted in the classroom and home setting (See Barclay, 1999).

Pertaining to Scientific Journals, Beckstead (2008) wrote:

Because every writing assignment occurred at the end of a science unit and required inclusion of scientific concepts covered in the unit, our scientific journals were an excellent form of assessment. Through these types of writing, a teacher can learn many things about the student's understanding of the concepts covered in a unit of study. By reading a student's essay, poem, or letter, the teacher can determine if a student needs clarification of any misconceptions they may have. These articles also help a teacher determine if a concept needs to be re-taught. . . .

Evaluation is an important responsibility of the science teacher. The teacher must use quality procedures to ascertain how well each student is doing in science. Instruction might well improve by using feedback from evaluation results. Metacognition is then involved.

In Conclusion

The mentor has salient responsibilities in developing quality science teachers. These teachers need to have adequate knowledge and skills pertaining to selecting objectives, learning activities and evaluation procedures in ongoing science units of study.

REFERENCES

Barclay, D. (1999), Making the Connections: Science and Literacy," *Childhood Education*, 75 (3), 146-152.

Beckstead, Larissa (2008), "Scientific Journals," *Science and Children*, 46 (3), 22-26.

Ediger, Marlow (2007), "Teacher Observation to Assess Student Achievement," *Journal of Instructional Psychology*, 34 (1), 137-139.

Ediger, Marlow (2007), "The Substitute Teacher in Reading Instruction," *The SubJournal*, 8 (2), 67-73.

Ediger, Marlow, and D. Bhaskara Rao (2007), *School Science Education*. New Delhi, India: Discovery Publishing House (Ltd.), p. 5.

Fitzhugh, Will (2006), "Where's the Content?" *Educational Leadership*, 64 (2), 42-47.

National Research Council (1996), National Science Education Standards (1996). Washington, DC: National Academy Press.

21 The New Science Teacher in the School Setting

The new science teacher needs monitoring to adjust well to the school setting. He/she must receive the assistance necessary to do well in science teaching. Feelings of uncertainty and anxiety need to be minimized as much as possible. The new teacher needs to be orientated to the school. How might the mentor/teacher relationship assist to make for a productive life in teaching and learning situations as a science teacher?

Mentoring and the New Science Teacher

The new science teacher must develop feelings of wanting to obtain needed knowledge about the local school and also about becoming a true professional. Thus, the mentor, among other things, may help the science teacher to:

- locate science equipment and materials.
- know other teachers in the school setting.
- find common supplies for use in teaching.
- become familiar with the school library.
- understand how the school schedule is organized.
- know rules and regulations for mandated testing.
- organize the classroom for science teaching (See Wessler, 2008).

Having graduated from an accredited university, the science teacher is ready to pursue actual teaching experiences.

In the pre-service experiences, the future teacher did indepth course work in science content involving earth, biological, and physical sciences. Applying the content areas, he/she engaged in pre-service experiences with public school students in observation of classroom activities pertaining to teaching and learning. Here, the regular teacher served as a role model and assisted the pre-service teacher in working with students individually as well as in small groups. These activities, for example, included students:

- designing and making posters involving conservation of natural resources.
- reading science subject matter from the basal text.
- assisting students in mastering vocabulary terms.
- helping learners in peer committee discussions.
- constructing a model soil conservation grassed waterway.
- demonstrating a science experiment (See Noddings, 2008).

The early field experiences provided readiness for student teaching. In student teaching, the future teacher experienced the entire scope and sequence of classroom teaching. Thus, he/she with cooperating teacher assistance did the following in student teaching:

- developed and introduced a science unit on "The Changing of the Earth's Surface" in large group instruction.
- organized followup small groups in extending topics presented in large group instruction such as (*a*) erosion of top soil, (*b*) terracing (*c*) planting trees for wind breaks (*d*) and seeding grass.
- assisted pupils to develop individual projects based on the science unit title, such as locating and presenting information on a self chosen topic, doing an art project and making a model, among others, decided upon through teacher/pupil planning (See Mesa, *et al.*, 2008).

To provide readiness for engaging pupils in each of the above named tasks, the student teacher and the cooperating teacher cooperatively showed and discussed a video tape dealing with changes occurring on the earth's surface including earthquakes, volcanic eruptions, tornados, as well as floods and mud slides. To work effectively in committees, pupils practiced using recommended guidelines for small group work. These include that every one participates actively, stays on the topic, gives everyone a chance to participate and emphasizes politeness in ongoing experiences (Ediger, 2008).

There are different reasons why science teachers are successful as compared those who lack these traits. The personality of the teacher is important. Thus, the teacher needs to be kind and highly accepting of others. This is modeled in situations involving committee endeavors in science. Rudeness and being inconsiderate are not characteristics which are admired by others. Values possessed by the teacher may well make for a good teacher. Believing in hard work is a value and this guides teachers in teaching and learning situations. Pupils are then evaluated based on effort put forth such as in doing a science experiment. Slovenly, careless work is not tolerated, but the best needs to go into student endeavors. Science teachers must present models for learner emulation in personality development and values (well prepared and taught lessons) put forth. Good teaching, too, may be considered as being learned behavior. Here, the science teacher studies and practices quality teaching endeavors in each day of instruction. This approach may soon become habitual and provide exemplars of excellence in teaching (See National Research Council, 1996).

According to Kennedy (2006), schools and districts can indeed improve teaching and they can do so in at least three different ways. They can improve the hiring procedures by reducing the time they spend on interviews and increasing the time they spend watching candidate videotapes. They can improve their professional development by reducing the money they spend on programs that offer bromides and exhortations and increasing the money they spend on para-professionals and on programs that address the real nuts and bolts of teaching. And they can improve their standard operating procedures so that they stop interfering with good teaching and start facilitating it.

The important lesson here is to think not just about teacher quality but also on teaching quality. Teaching is inherently an unpredictable, complex enterprise. But we are making it far more unpredictable than it has to be with policies and practices that go in the way of high quality teaching and learning.

There may be students who do not achieve as optimally as they are capable and may be labelled as being under-achievers. Each student needs to achieve as optimally as possible. New science teachers need to possess vital guidelines which assist in teaching and learning situations. Kumar, *et al.,* (2008) provide the following for assisting learners individually to attain as well as possible:

- provide consistent and constructive feedback.
- give choices, focus on interests.
- vary teaching styles to accommodate learning styles.
- provide for active and experimental learning.
- use mentorship and role models.
- adopt education that is relevant and personally meaningful; an education that provides insight and self understanding.
- have nurturing, affirming classrooms.

New science teachers then need guidance in providing the best science curriculum possible, using strategies of instruction which motivate each learner. Engaging students to achieve, develop and grow in goal attainment is salient. Science learning activities need to be challenging and yet make for enjoyment in achieving knowledge, skills and attitudinal objectives. Understanding new facts, concepts and generalizations propels the student in wanting to learn with intrinsic motivation being in evidence. Purpose, or reasons for learning, increases the motivational level of the student in ongoing science lessons and units of study. Individual differences among students need adequate provision so that successful achievers in science is possible (Ediger and Rao, 2007).

The New Teacher in the Instructional Arena

With adequate background information at his/her disposal, the new science teacher generally needs gradual induction into the regular classroom. Depending upon the revealed capabilities in science teaching, the amount of mentor assistance will vary from teacher to teacher. The heart of the science curriculum is doing experiments. Students must be actively involved in science experimentation. Motivating learners in desiring to do experiments needs to be emphasized with interesting readiness experiences. Careful observation by all is salient when the experiment is ongoing. Learners need to develop and then test an hypothesis. Objective thinking from students is wanted. Extended learnings from the experiment include:

- reading from a variety of related sources, including the internet, to confirm or refute the findings.
- doing a research project such as using the project method to incorporate hands on learning approaches.
- writing up each experiment, using proper style and grammar which is appropriate for the developmental level of the student. A bound volume may be made of these write ups.
- observing and summarizing related video tapes with summarizing statements being placed in a student developed journal.
- working in a peer setting to summarize and assess several agreed upon library books on science directly related to the ongoing science unit of study.

In Closing

Perhaps, the best way to conclude this manuscript is to quote the following criteria as to the main characteristics of science:

1. Science proceeds on the assumptions, based upon centuries of experience, that the universe is not capricious.
2. Science knowledge is based on observation of samples of matter that are accessible to public investigation in contrast to purely private inspection.
3. Science aims at achieving a systematic and comprehensive understanding of various sectors or aspects of nature.
4. Science is not and probably never will be a finished enterprise and there remains very much more to be discovered about how things in the universe behave and how they are inter-related.
5. Measurement is an important feature of most branches of modern science because of the formation as well as the establishment of laws facilitated through the development of quantitative distinctions (Seeniammal, 2007).

REFERENCES

Ediger, Marlow (2008), "The School and Students in Society," *Journal of Instructional Psychology*, 35 (3), 260-263.

Ediger, Marlow and Digumarti Bhaskara Rao (2007), *Science Curriculum and Instruction*. New Delhi, India: Discovery Publishing House (Ltd.).

Kennedy, Mary M. (2006), "From Teacher Quality to Teaching Quality," *Educational Leadership*, 63 (6), 14-19.

Kumar, M. Suresh, *et al.*, (2008), "Reversing the Underachievement of School Students through Motivational Strategies," *Edutracks*, 8 (2) 16-17.

Mesa, Jennifer C., *et al.*, (2008), "The P.O.E.T.R.Y Of Science," *Science and Children*, 46 (3), 36-41.

National Research Council (1996), *National Science Education Standards*, Washington, DC: National Academy Press.

Noddings, Nel (2008), "Schooling for Democracy," *Phi Delta Kappan*, 90 (1), 34-37.

Seeniammal, V. (2007) A Study of Problems of High School and Higher Secondary School Students in Learning Chemistry in Tirunelveli District, Ph D thesis appraised by Marlow Ediger for VOC College of Education, Centre for Research in Education, Tamil Nadu, India (page 6) with recognition for these standards going to The National Science Teacher's Association, Washington, DC.

Wessler, Stephen (2008), "Civility Speaks Up," *Educational Leadership* 66 (1), 44-48.

The Substitute Teacher in Science

Too frequently when the regular teacher is absent due to illness or bereavement in the family among other reasons, students in the classroom are taught by someone poorly prepared for teaching science. The term "baby sitting" is generally applied to these situations. Must it be that way? The answer is a resounding "no!" School districts need to provide paid inservice education for those desiring to substitute teach in science. When absences occur of the regular teacher, the substitute teacher needs to play the role of a qualified science teacher in assisting students to achieve as optimally as possible. Sequence in student science achievement is hindered with substitute teachers who merely are present in the classroom and do not engage learners in ongoing lessons and units of study (Ediger and Rao, 2007).

Inservice Education and the Substitute Teacher

The substitute teacher needs assistance from a lead teacher or science supervisor to be fully cognizant of the duties and responsibilities of teaching science. The basal science textbook, the course of study, lesson plans, and designed units of study, along with being introduced to the materials of instruction, provide a basis for the inservice education program (Ediger, 2007).

The subteacher needs orientation as to what is the heart of the science curriculum, namely experimentation. He/she should observe how experiments fit into each lesson/unit of study. Experimentation is integrated, not a separate entity. Prior to an experiment, students need to possess adequate readiness to benefit from the learning activity. Looking at and discussing a related videotape will assist in providing readiness in that necessary knowledge and skills are then activated (National Research Council, 1996).

Students need to observe the experiment carefully and not jump to hasty conclusions. Objective information is a requirement. Opinions and subjective ideas are treated as hypotheses and are tested in the experiment. Results from the experiment are corroborated/refuted with additional research. The one variable, alone, must be tested in the experiment. Extraneous factors need to be eliminated. The subteacher, too, needs to be highly knowledgeable of data sources to check the results of an experiment or to extend knowledge about related concepts and generalizations. These include the following using:

- internet and world wide web sources.
- up to date trade books, basal science series and science encyclopedias.
- DVDs containing relevant and reliable information.
- information from a nearby university science professor or other science teachers in the school setting.
- a redoing of the original experiment (See Wenglinsky, 2006).

The subteacher needs to understand what is meant by learnings being developmentally appropriate for a student. Quality sequence is not possible in teaching and learning situations unless the activities and experiences are challenging and yet optimal achievement is possible. With high expectations for each student and success in learning being in evidence, the science teacher might well feel successful in teaching. Student learning and understanding is attached to what is being learned. It is highly significant for students to perceive purpose in learning. Reasons for active involvement in ongoing lessons and units of study are then being stressed. The science teacher may state a purpose or students, periodically, may brainstorm reasons for participating in an ongoing topic. Thus, purposes should exist for student participation in:

- a problem solving activity such as in an experiment. The problem, an hypothesis, and a conclusion must be garnered by students with teacher guidance.
- a project method which involves student cooperative planning with teacher assistance. The project may, for example, deal with research on alternative sources of energy or how a home/school may conserve on energy consumption.
- a construction activity which night even provide an example for a local science fair (See Zales and Unger, 2008).

Additional Needs of the Subteacher

The subteacher must be conscious of reading needs of students in in ongoing science lessons. These needs pertain to:

- word recognition assistance.
- comprehension strategies with cause/effect as well as a critical and creative reading emphasis.

Evaluation needs to be continuous using teacher observation, teacher written tests with appropriate validity and reliability and performance tasks being stressed (Ediger, 2007).

In Closing

Subteachers need to provide a quality science curriculum with the best objectives, learning activities and appraisal techniques being used. High, reasonable expectations for student achievement need to be in the offing. Each student must achieve optimally in science!

REFERENCES

Ediger, Marlow (2007), "Learning Activities in the Curriculum," *College Student Journal*, 41 (40), 967-969.

Ediger, Marlow (2007), "The Substitute Teacher in Reading Instruction," *SubJournal*, 8 (2), 67-73.

Ediger, Marlow and Digumarti Bhaskara Rao (2007), *School Science Education*. New Delhi, India: Discovery Publishing House (Ltd.).

National Research Council (1996), *National Science Education Standards*. Washington, DC: National Academy Press.

Wenglinsky, Harold (2005-2006), "Technology and Achievement: The Bottom Line," *Educational Leadership*, 63 (4), 29-33.

Zales, Charlotte Rapper, and Connie W. Unger (2008), "The Science and Literacy Framework," *Science and Children*, 46 (3), 42-45.

23 The School Principal as Science Supervisor

Science supervision may come from several resource personnel. In the elementary/middle school level, the principal may assume that responsibility. He/she must be well-versed pertaining to trends in science teaching. Continually studying what makes for an effective science curriculum is a must! The principal has numerous opportunities to observe quality science instruction when making observational visits to different classrooms. Ideas gleaned may be passed on to other teachers. The principal needs to not only encourage good science teaching but also must motivate teachers in the school setting to share ideas and assist other teachers to teach effectively and well. Thus, there are several resources to use in developing excellence in the science curriculum (Ediger and Rao, 2007).

Criteria for School Administrators to Emphasize

There are several guidelines which school administrators need to stress in working with teachers to improve science instruction. Thus, teachers need to engage pupils in learning. Too many pupils are turned off or fail to achieve in an ongoing lesson. These pupils must be identified and brought into the teaching/learning act. A different kind of learning experience in science may assist to develop interest within these learners to achieve. Teacher observation needs to be utilized to notice which pupils might benefit from these changes (See Maheshwari, 2009).

Second, pupils need to make sense pertaining to what was taught. Memorizing meaningless materials for a test has meager benefits for the learner. The learner must understand presented facts, concepts and generalizations in order to use these as building blocks for ensuing lessons. Meaning exists within the mind of the learner. The teacher's role is to assist pupils to understand and use what was achieved. Meaningful explanations, learning opportunities and feedback from appraisal results, might well help the pupil to achieve at higher levels. New learnings are built upon those acquired previously. Pupils need to raise questions pertaining to what is not comprehended and thus arrive at meaning in the science curriculum.

Third, the school principal must stress pupil purpose in learning when helping teachers develop skill in teaching. With purpose, reasons exist within the pupil in acquisition of knowledge, skills and attitudes. A low level of motivation results if a pupil cannot sense reasons for achieving vital scientific information. The teacher may very briefly explain, deductively, the purpose or reason for pupils participating in a given science learning activity. Or, inductively pupils may understand the purpose with a series of questions raised by the teacher as to why a specific science activity is necessary to pursue. Motivation might then well increase (See NSTA Reports, 2009).

Fourth, pupils achieve at different levels and possess diverse styles of learning, individually. Thus, the teacher must use concrete (the outdoors, excursions, objects and items), the semi-concrete (video tapes, illustrations, computers, slides, and multi-media in general), as well as abstract (listening, speaking, reading and writing activities), in providing for individual differences in the classroom. Different ways of grouping pupils for instruction, also, must be emphasized, such as homogeneous, heterogeneous, the class as a whole, committee endeavors, and individual study as means of grouping pupils for instruction (See National Research Council, 2000).

Observational Visits in Classrooms

The school principal needs to observe science teachers teach in the classroom. There are numerous recommendations which principals may make as a result of these observational visits. Each recommendation is made in order to improve science instruction. The following observations made should be followed with recommendations for improved instruction:

- few pupils are able to see, clearly, the science experiment being performed. Materials used should be arranged in a place whereby observations by all pupils may readily be made. Small groups, in sequence, may need to observe an experiment at a given time. Readiness for the ensuing experiment must be in evidence so that pupils may relate the ensuing with previous learnings acquired. Otherwise optimal learning may not take place. Jumping too far ahead of pupils makes for frustration in achieving whereas experiments performed which are too easy to comprehend might well make for boredom. Experimentation should fascinate learners and foster an inward desire to learn (Ediger, 2008).
- selected pupils are left out of discussions. There may be too few actively participating and yet all need to be actively engaged in the discussion. The science teacher needs to motivate each pupil to participate. No one should be ridiculed for participating, but rather all should be encouraged. The self concept is involved in assisting all pupils to be successful in the discussion setting. The class as a whole as well as small group discussions need to be in the offing. The latter helps more pupils to feel free to participate. The self confidence of each must be strengthened so all have salient contributions to make (See David, 2008).
- some may not wish to participate in an ongoing learning opportunity. These need to be identified and motivated to perform. This must be approached cautiously with feelings of success experienced by these learners. No

doubt non-contributors have experienced failure too frequently. It might be, also, that these pupils do not understand what is being taught. Reading activities in science do cause difficulties for some pupils. Word recognition problems and difficulties in fluent reading are hindrances in comprehending ideas being read (See Pardo, 2004).

- mainstreamed pupils with different disabilities need to be accepted as humans having much worth. They need encouragement to use talents and abilities possessed. Strengths and hobbies need to be brought into the science curriculum. Subject matter discussed may be brought in to their understanding level in small group sessions. No one should experience rudeness or shunning.

Diagnosis for not understanding relevant facts, concepts, and generalizations must be noted and remedied with appropriate learning activities. No child should fall through the slats. Science literacy for all is needed and each learner should attain optimally.

Using Computer Technology in the Classroom

There are a plethora of ways in which pupils may use computer services in the science curriculum. A dictionary, a thesaurus, an encyclopedia, and the word processor itself are tools for learning in ongoing science lessons and units of study. An electronic portfolio is an excellent means of showing achievement for parents, teachers, school administrators, among other responsible people, to notice a child's sequential progress. Here, the pupil with teacher assistance may select what to enter into the computer to show representative progress in science. In the past portfolios have been used to also show a representative sampling of a pupil's progress, but not with computer use. In an electronic portfolio, the pupil may enter the following dated entries in science:

- a book report related directly to subject matter discussed in an ongoing science unit of study such as on prehistoric life in the Mesozoic Era.

- a summary on a video tape viewed such as Hurricanes and Tornados.
- conclusions reached from a large group session on invertebrates.
- electronic pictures taken for a bulletin board display developed on opaque, transparent and translucent materials.
- a mural made on igneous, sedimentary and metamorphic rocks.
- impressions acquired from a unit on sustainable, non-polluting sources of energy.
- a write up on an individual self chosen project made pertaining to magnetism and electricity (Ediger, 2006).

The word processor may be used to keep a running record of diary entries kept for each science unit studied. The daily entries need to be dated and each happening recorded accurately and clearly. This activity can easily move into the direction of pupils doing scientific journals. Beckstead (2009) wrote the following:

> Having my students create science journals doesn't happen during the first week of school. The students need to have data and other information recorded in their science journals in order to order to be able to create science journals. A good place to start is our rocks and minerals unit. During this unit, students observe different kinds of rocks and do different types of tests on the rocks, go on a rock hunt. . . All observations are recorded in their science notebooks.

But we are still not ready to create the journal. Not only does the science have to be taught, but also certain writing and grammar skills have to be taught and developed before students write articles, stories and poems for a science journal.

The science journal is used, along with other procedures, to appraise learner progress in science. Parents, the school principal, the involved pupil and the science teacher may use the science journal not only to assess but also to report learner progress. Continuous efforts must be made in using modern technology to assist pupils in achieving more optimally in science.

The science teacher always needs to be on the lookout for ways to incorporate computer technology into the science curriculum. It might well be a motivator for learning involving pupils.

Evaluation of Achievement in Science

The school principal has numerous responsibilities as curriculum supervisor to inform teachers on methods of appraising pupil achievement. Thus, he/she needs to assist teachers to understand the following concepts:

- **Validity:** Examples need to be given here in that a test is valid if it measures what it is supposed to measure. Thus, if x is to be measured in pupil achievement, the test items then must relate directly to x.
- **Reliability:** Here, a test must measure consistently and not fluctuate in test results for a pupil from one testing to the next for the same test. Test/ratest, as well as split half reliability, may also be stressed.
- **Standard Deviation:** This indicates how pupil's test scores deviate from the mean. One standard deviation above the mean represents 34.13 per cent of those taking the test, whereas 34.13 per cent of pupils are below the mean of the total number tested being one standard deviation below the mean.
- **Percentiles:** Percentiles show the range of pupil's test scores from the first to the 99th percentile. Thus, for example, if a pupil received a hypothetical score of 36, he/she would be on the 60th percentile; out of every 100 pupils taking the test, forty would be above and sixty below that hypithetical score. The raw score of 36 was compared to a Table which gave the percentile results for the test.

The above-named four measurement concepts are used very commonly in mandated testing whereby the mean of all scores is tabulated as well as the standard deviation and percentiles. Percentiles do not mean the per cent answered correctly by a pupil on a test but rather, but rather how he/ she compares with others when converting a raw score to a standard score (See National Research Council, 1996).

REFERENCES

Beckstead, Larissa (2009), "Scientific Journals, A Creative Assessment Tool," *Science and Children*, 46 (3), 22-23.

David, Jane (2008), "Project Based Learning", *Educational Leadership*, 65 (5), 80-84.

Ediger, Marlow (2006), "Testing Versus Portfolios to Assess Achievement," *OASCD Journal*, 13 (1), 31-32.

Ediger, Marlow (2008), "Leadership in the School Setting," *Education*, 129 (1), 17-20.

Ediger, Marlow and Digumarti Bhaskara Rao (2007), *School Science Education*. New Delhi, India: Discovery Publishing House.

Maheshwari, Amrita (2009), "Integral Values of Science Education," *Edutracks*, 8 (4), 16-17.

National Research Council (NRC), *National Science Education Standards* (1996). Washington, DC: National Academy Press.

National Research Council (2000), *How Pupils Learn*. Washington, DC: National Academy Press.

NSTA Reports (2009), National Science Teachers Association. Washington DC: NSTA.

Pardo, Laura (2004), "What Every Teacher Needs to Know About Comprehension," *The Reading Teacher*, 58 (3), 272-283.

Mathematics
Content and Pedagogy

The debate has gone on for some time in terms of which is more salient for the teacher to be well versed in mathematical content versus methods and approaches in teaching. Both are salient. They cannot be separated from each other. The mathematics teacher must indeed have broad, indepth knowledge of subject matter as well as in teaching and learning. Mathematical content and pedagogy then need to be integrated. The goal of mathematics teachers is to assist pupils to achieve, grow, and develop in attaining vital facts, concepts, and generalizations. This takes teacher knowledge of content as weli as of pedagogy.

Teaching of Mathematics

There are several needs of individuals in becoming proficient in mathematics. Thus, each person needs to be able to use mathematics in everyday transactions such as buying necessary goods and services. To buy groceries, pay utility bills and rent, and pay for needed services such as repairs and maintenance work. Functioning well, numerically, in society is a need for all citizens. Then too, a mathematics curriculum must provide for those going into higher education and will major in and teach mathematics. Also, there will be future engineers and other professionals who need to experience a high quality school curriculum. Individual differences then must be provided for in the elementary and secondary school years. Sequentially, pupils need to experience teachers who possess ample knowledge of subject matter as well as of methods of teaching mathematics (Ediger and Rao, 2000).

Quality teachers are needed, as a key ingredient, in assisting optimal pupil learning. They must experience the latest, relevant trends in teaching mathematics, be it in workshops, other inservice education programs, or through personal research projects. Cooperation among teachers to conduct grade level meetings as well as school wide, and system wide endeavors at curriculum improvement should provide for provisions made for optimal achievement in mathematics of each learner. Here, content and pedagogy need integration in helping pupils achieve well. The two should not be separated from each other, nor should value judgments be made as to which is more important (Ediger, 2005).

Mathematics as a language needs to be used to communicate ideas. Communication must occur in school and in society between and among individuals pertaining to quantitative topics. Precision is involved. Mathematics is perhaps the most objective of all academic disciplines whereby individuals agree, as a whole, with the quantity being discussed. It attempts to be precise with the quantity being considered. Among others, mathematical ideas may be expressed orally and in diagrams, charts, tables, formulas, library books, graphs and written work (See Betne and Castonguay, 2008).

Pupils need to make connections in terms of use of mathematical subject matter. They need to perceive how mathematics relates to the self, as well as others. Problem solving is a vital skill for all to develop. Developmentally and at increasing levels of difficulty, pupils must be able to solve personal mathematics problems. Logical thinking is necessary here as well as dealing factually with quantitative information. Critical thinking is inherent when separating facts from opinions, the relevant from the non-relevant, as well as fantasy from reality in problem solving experiences. Creative thinking, too, is necessary in determining new methods of solving a problem. Novel, unique ways of viewing and attempting solutions at problem solving are to be encouraged (See Stein, 2007).

Contextual situations are needed in fostering the utilization of mathematics. Standardized tests stress the application of mathematics outside the framework of a particular context. Pupils then respond to test items which do not pinpoint a functional use. Then too, pupils are drilled much to do well on a standardized test. Generally, drill assists pupils in turning off in studying mathematics. Mathematics can be made into a fascinating academic discipline with the solving of life like problems whereby pupils may see its use in society. Challenging and interesting methods may be used to stimulate pupil interest in learning mathematics. Mathematics certainly need not be dull and uninteresting. Actually, it should be enjoyable and fascinating. New objectives need to be built upon what pupils have learned previously (See National Council Teachers of Mathematics, 2000).

There are diverse kinds of knowledge that teachers need to teach mathematics to pupils and include knowledge of:

- subject matter including important principles and meanings, formulas, facts, processes and procedures, rules, definitions, as well as structural ideas.
- pedagogy such as lesson and unit planning and implementation, questions to ask and problems to solve, explanations to use, examples to provide as in diagrams and formulas and demonstrations to make situations meaningful and concrete.
- pedagogical subject matter including determining prerequisites pupils possess prior to instruction, sequence used to develop vital mathematical understandings among learners, diagnosis of pupil difficulties in learning, as well as strategies to use with quality materials of instruction (See Jeyanthi, 2008).
- information about pupils in the classroom. Here, the teacher needs to understand the developmental level of each pupil and where he/she is achieving presently. The teacher should not impart content too difficult,

nor to easy for learner attainment. Thus, the subject matter to be imparted needs to be challenging, yet achievable. The learning styles of pupils need to be considered in teaching and learning situations. Thus, a pupil may prefer direct teaching of content as compared to learning by discovery. He/she may prefer to work by the self instead of in collaborative situations. Then too, pupils may prefer a textbook approach as compared to more open ended procedures in using a variety of activities and experiences.

- curriculum development curriculum practices and procedures. Mathematics teachers need to develop proficiency in writing cognitive, psychomotor and affective objectives for pupil attainment. These must be written in measurable terms to ascertain if they have/have not been achieved by learners. Diagnosis is then possible to determine which learning activities are necessary for pupils to remedy deficits. A variety of valid, reliable measurement procedures need to be used to determine pupil progress. Multiple choice and essay test items, among others may then be emphasized (See National Council Teachers of Mathematics, 1989).

The mathematics teacher then must appraise the self to notice if there are personal strengths in mathematics to effectively emphasize the scope and sequence of needed math in the curriculum to teach effectively. Inservice education may take care of deficiencies since what is not known may not be taught or be taught well for pupil understanding and meaning. The goal of teachers here should be to obtain a master's degree in mathematics as a minimum. Online education is also possible to work at home, at one's own convenience, in taking additional course work in mathematics knowledge and pedagogy. School sponsored workshops and attending professional meetings, are further avenues of inservice education. The principles of educational psychology must be stressed adequately in course work dealing with imparting mathematical knowledge to pupils (See Hyde, 2006).

The Attitudinal Dimension in Teaching Mathematics

The self concept of the teacher is of utmost importance. He/she must believe in the worth of the individual. This is true in believing in one self as well as in others. The following traits of teachers are salient when thinking of teaching mathematics:

- possessing a good attitude toward mathematics as an academic discipline.
- having positive attitudes toward teaching in general and teaching mathematics, in particular.
- inculcating a philosophy of teaching which accepts research results as a guide to teaching.
- enjoying mathematics as an area of study as well as in imparting knowledge, skills and attitudes toward pupils.
- wanting to become increasingly proficient in teaching mathematics.
- desiring to attend workshop sessions, to take courses in mathematics/pedagogy, as well as in the psychology of teaching and learning.
- emphasizing a positive relationship with parents in assisting their offspring to do well in mathematics, as well as in school in general.

The attitudinal dimension is further emphasized in classroom management procedures. The mathematics teacher must have a quality classroom environment for teaching and learning. Pupils are respected and yet learners are mannerly when relating to others. The teacher has reasonable expectations from pupils in goal attainment. Successful achievement is salient for each pupil. Teachers are able to work well with pupils in large group, cooperative endeavors and in individualized instruction. Emotional achievement is important for every one in the classroom, in school and in society (See Glatthorn and Fox, 1996).

REFERENCES

Betne, Praha, and Remi Castonguay (2008), "On the Role of Mathematics Educators and Librarians in Constructive Pedagogy," *Education*, 129 (1), 56-79.

Ediger, Marlow (2005), "Teaching Mathematics in the High School Setting," *College Student Journal*, 39 (4), 711-715.

Ediger, Marlow, and D. Bhaskara Rao (2000), *Teaching Mathematics Successfully*. New Delhi, India: Discovery Publishing House.

Glatthorn, A. A., and L. E. Fox (1996), *Quality Teaching Through Professional Development*. Thousand Oaks, CA: Corwin Press.

Hyde, A. A. (2006), *Comprehending Math: Adapting Strategies to Teach Mathematics K-6*. Portsmouth, NH: Heinemann.

Jeyanthi, S. (2008), Cognitive and Attitudinal Correlates of Teaching Performance of B. Ed. Mathematics Teachers. Kodaikanal, India: Mother Teresa Women's University, 41-48. Ph D thesis appraised by Marlow Ediger in serving as an External Examiner for Mother Teresa University.

National Council Teachers of Mathematics (1989), *Curriculum and Evaluation Standards for School Mathematics*. Reston, Va.: NCTM.

National Council Teachers of Mathematics (2000), *Principles and Standards for School Mathematics*. Reston, Va.: NCTM.

Stein, Lynn Arthur (2007), "How Mathematics Counts," *Educational Leadership*, 65 (3), 9-14.

Mathematics, the Learner and the Curriculum

There is a long history of mathematics instruction beginning with Colonial America schools. Most teachers at that time (1607-1776) stressed rote learning of basic addition, subtraction, multiplication, and division facts. These were printed by the teacher on large slate/chalkboards and then pupils copied each on their smaller slateboards. Drill was not an exactly interesting method of teaching and physical punishment was used by many colonial teachers to "motivate" pupils. Christopher Dock, a Mennonite Teacher, was an exception in that he stressed kindness and patience in teaching. He did use physical punishment, sparingly, as a last resort. Religious beliefs then tended to emphasize pupils being born in sin and the evilness needed to be driven out of individuals.

After the colonial period of time, there were numerous advocates for change in teaching ands learning situations. In the early 1800s, Joseph Lancaster and his Monitorial System was brought to the United States. Lancaster, among other things, stressed a certain sequence in arithmetic when teaching pupils by monitors under the supervision of the head teacher. He arranged arithmetic in terms of the following order being followed in teaching: simple addition, followed by compound addition where carrying was involved, simple subtraction, compound subtraction which stressed the concept of borrowing, simple multiplication, compound multiplication, and simple division followed by compound division. Each division of arithmetic was taught in isolation. Thus, for example, addition and subtraction were unrelated. Rote learning and memorization were still the methods of teaching utilized. Slates continued to be used by pupils to copy number pairs for purposes of drill and practice. More modern practices of teaching came to the shores of the United States with the advent of Johann Friedrich Pestalozzi's object lesson of instruction. In arithmetic, Pestalozzi (1746-1827) emphasized that objects be used in arithmetic such as in counting, addition, subtraction, multiplication, as well as in division. Thus, in addition, a certain number of objects were joined to another group, resulting in addition. This made arithmetic much more meaningful, of course, as compared to memorizing basic facts. Friedrich Froebel (1782-1852) contributed much on kindergarden level of education. One set of arithmetic materials were called "gifts," and consisted of cubes, blocks, points, line segments, spheres and cylinders. Play was stressed as a method of education and pupils made diverse designs from these materials; mathematics was understandable through seeing first hand the different objects in doing the four basic operations on number. Froebel considered the sphere as the perfect symbol since there were no edges; he frequently emphasized mathematical designs in his writings. The utilization of mother play songs were stressed in Froebel's kindergarten with pupils standing in a circle and creatively dramatizing what was sung, a far cry from Colonial schools of rote learning and (Ediger and Rao, 1982).

Standards in Teaching Mathematics

Mathematics teachers must stay abreast of updated ideas in subject matter and skills in teaching and learning situations. This is true regardless of national and state standards being emphasized in the curriculum. The focal point must be the pupil in developing a learner centered procedure of instruction. Thus, the teacher needs to have the pupil involved in designing each lesson and unit of study. First of all, each objective stressed must be challenging and yet attainable. If challenge is not involved, boredom might well set in and achievement goes downhill, whereas unachievable objectives are indeed frustrating and might well aid in pupils in giving up in whole or in part. The latter may be avoidable through scaffolding whereby the mathematics teacher orders questions which stress learner responses until the objective has been attained. If objectives are too easy and require little/no effort for pupils to achieve, adjustments may be added to emphasize more rigor in the curriculum. By studying each learner and having as much knowledge about him/her as possible, the teacher has a better basis for decision making. Thus the interests, hobbies, home background including the number and relationship of siblings, parental level of education as well as aspirations for the child and general economic status, assist the mathematics teacher in understanding each learner more effectively. This knowledge must be utilized to provide for individual differences among pupils.

Second, culture helps in shaping an individual. The writer when teaching in a two teacher school in the middle 1950s had several Holdeman Mennonite children in his classroom. The boys, in particular, took much interest in arithmetic and little in social studies. Eighth grade education was terminal and farming was going to be the way of life. At that time, the basal arithmetic textbook still had numerous problems dealing with farm related items such as, "Given the dimensions of a grain bin (diameter and height), how my bushels of wheat would the bin hold?" Each bushel averaged 60 pounds. When the writer was in the intermediate and upper grades in a rural school during the middle 1930s and early 40s, memorization of pounds per bushel of grain for wheat, oats, barley, corn, and sorghum was stressed when society was much more rural as compared to presently when less than 2 per cent of the population make their living from farming. Even then there are farmers of the 2 per cent who have a job in a nearby rural city. Thus, in our schools of today, there must be a culture of achievement in mathematics, among other subject matter areas. High standards are set with related expectations for achievement of objectives of instruction; these standards/expectations must be attainable, not frustrating (Ediger, and Rao, 2012).

Third, readiness for ensuing leanings in mathematics must be emphasized by all teachers. Each new lesson stresses challenging concepts and generalizations to be learned. Background subject matter which engages pupils then relates directly to the new lesson. Already in the 1800s, Johann Friedrich Herbart (1776-1841) in his laboratory schools for training teachers emphasized five steps to be followed in each lesson plan. These were preparation (developing pupil readiness to benefit from the ensuing lesson); presentation (presenting the new concepts and generalizations); association (relating the new learnings with that stressed in the readiness activities); generalization (Drawing conclusions from step three in relating the new with the old); and use (applying what had been learned). Thus, selected main ideas have been developed from Herbart's model which tends to have some relevancy today, especially in providing readiness for ensuing leanings to be acquired in mathematics. Then too, learners must have ample opportunities to utilize subject matter so that it is not forgotten and it remains in the repertoire of pupils. Too frequently, content is memorized and learned for test taking; more important, pupils need to make practical and abstract use of mathematical ideas in school and in society.

Fourth, learners must leam from each other as well as from the teacher. Here, pupils need to have chances to work collaboratively. Thus, pupils can learn from each other in committee settings. Being able to work harmoniously with others is vital in the societal setting. Disharmony, rudeness, and quarreling make for unhealthy environments. Rather focusing attention on a problem to be solved makes for higher levels of cognition. Pupils contribute to solutions to be found in mathematics. Vygotsky (1933,1978) advocated that learning is a social situation and occurs when pupils' ideas "bounce off each others minds." Committee work then becomes highly significant whereby subject matter is shared, as well as conclusions reached collaboratively. This still leaves time in daily endeavors for pupils working individually. The preferred style of learning, also, is involved here in that selected pupils prefer working with others to achieve more optimally as compared to those attaining more in working by the self.

Fifth, not only should the mathematics curriculum be learner centered, but also adequate focus must be made toward attaining objectives of instruction. Thus, purpose in obtaining each objective must be felt by learners. Time spent by the mathematics teachers in assisting learners to perceive reasons for learning is time well spent. For each lesson presentation, the teacher needs to provide reasons for studying subject matter; this can be done inductively whereby pupils discover purpose for attaining worthwhile subject matter. Promoting perceived purpose energizes and provides a higher energy level for learning. Motivation for achievement might be a major problem for pupils, but there are a plethora of means to assist in becoming increasingly motivated.

Sixth, learning should be enjoyable and not a burden. Thus, learners need to experience poignant activities which encourage and help pupils achieve. There are a variety of kinds of activities available using concrete, semi-concrete, as well as abstract experiences. Video games are pleasant for many pupils and this type of technology must be available to learners. Challenging and interesting video games are a fascinating way of learning for those who like technology. In this modern age of technology, it is imperative that its use be made in today's world.

REFERENCES

Ediger, Marlow and D. Bhaskara Rao (1982), *Philosophy and Education*, New Delhi, India: Discovery Publishing House.

Ediger, Marlow and D. Bhaskara Rao (2012), *Essays in Teaching Mathematics*, New Delhi, India: Discovery Publishing House.

Vygotsky, Len (1933 and 1978), *Mind in Society*. Cambridge, Massachusetts: Harvard University Press.

Computer Aided Instruction in the Mathematics Curriculum

A very common approach of teaching mathematics emphasizes the use of a carefully chosen textbook as a guide to follow in student instruction. Diverse audio-visual aids may be used to enrich and clarify experiences. The methods of teaching used may incorporate deductive, inductive and problem solving procedures. Students are tested along the way with formative tests to indicate how well they have mastered the material at a given point in time. Ultimately, a summative test might well be given to notice learner progress and achievement for the entire unit of instruction. A mandated test may also be required to reveal how well the student is achieving the objectives of the local state. This in a nut shell describes the general way of mathematics instruction followed by classroom teachers. In contrast, the balance of this paper will discuss computer aided (CAI) instruction as well as elaborate on basal textbook procedures.

The Student and Computerized Instruction

In CAI, mathematics instruction is strongly geared to the individual student. Meeting the math needs of individual students must receive priority. Students need to pace learnings at their own unique optimal rate of achievement. The mathematical content must be relevant and useful in school and in society. A well developed program needs to be on the developmental level of the learner so that he/she may achieve as optimally as possible (Ediger and Rao, 2001).

The teacher needs to be passionate and enthusiastic about mathematics and the math curriculum. A conscientious indepth study of computerized programs/packages needs to be made to ascertain which are best suitable for a given set of learners, as well as for individual students. Careful consideration in selecting computer packages should follow the ensuing criteria:

- the level of mathematical content difficulty is appropriate for subject matter acquisition.
- math vocabulary terms assist students to attach meaning to ongoing experiences.
- accuracy of subject matter is inherent in each package and does not contain stereotypes offensive to any human being.
- purpose for each software package possesses clarity.
- quality sequence is emphasized in that students are successful achievers in its use.
- graphics, color and sound, promote the learning of mathematics.
- each program motivates students to achieve, grow and learn.
- feedback to learners' responses provides necessary and valuable information for the ensuing item to be learned (Djeassilane, 2008).

The above-named criteria provide guidance and direction in selecting software programs in mathematics for students to attain vital objectives of instruction. The subject matter content needs to be meaningful and understandable. The level of vocabulary difficulty must enable the learner to achieve in valuable mathematical knowledge. Each computer program needs to have content which meets the standard of being entirely accurate. The order of subject matter knowledge must be such that each student is successful in making progress. Challenging, but achievable content, needs to be in the offing. Peripherals must assist students to achieve and not hinder learner concentration on the task at hand. From test results, the student must receive usable feedback which promotes future learning. CAI programs may assist in evaluating student readiness for new learnings through pre-testing. Computerized subject matter content is then more likely to be presented in an achievable form. Drill items assist learners to retain knowledge. Drill needs to promote interest in learning and not minimize it. These programs may be game based drill items to assist learners to enjoy and appreciate mathematics. Post-test items are given to ascertain specifically what has been learned by students. Test information is then stored for future use by the mathematics teacher (Ediger, 2005).

CAI makes it possible to have self directed learning. The student then interacts with software in a computer. Responses that students make from content on the monitor provide data to the machine as to which subject matter comes next in sequence. The next sequential mathematical item should then be on the achievement level of the student. The opportunities to be a successful learner are indeed great. Without computerized math instruction, the teacher may move forward too rapidly or too slowly in aiding learner achievement, either through lecture or a discussion. In computerized math learnings, the next sequential item presented on the monitor is based on the level of success experienced in the previous item. Readiness for the ensuing learning is then based on previously acquired knowledge (Ediger, 2006).

There is efficiency in teaching when students experience much success in achieving knowledge goals in mathematics. Failure and mistakes are minimized. CAI never grows tired, nor disgusted with students in developing knowledge and skills. It promotes interaction between the computer and the student on an individualized basis, much like a tutor and a child. It is designed to meet the mathematical needs of a student. It is learner centered in providing for individual differences. The pace of learning is determined by the student (See National Council Teachers of Mathematics, 1989).

Feedback from test results assists pupils to notice progress and achievement. The learner then notices what needs further help in mathematics knowledge and skill. Diagnosis and prescription will assist the learner to remedy that which needs remediating so that further progress is in evidence. CAI, basically, is an automated method of teaching whereby the learner and the computer interact to achieve objectives of instruction. The following steps are followed in designing CAI programs:

- evaluating the present status of a student's achievement with a pre-test.
- providing mathematical subject matter in a meaningful manner.
- presenting drill and practice activities to fix knowledge in the mind of the learner.
- assisting pupil interest in learning with a gaming approach.
- assessing student achievement by using a post test.
- walking learners through a sequence of software teaching packages.
- keeping a record of test scores to notice student achievement (See Wiske, 2004).

CAI may emphasize simulations whereby a reality basis situation is placed into a computer program. Simulation might then be integrated with other less reality based programs that are abstract in nature. Simulation may show the stages of an insect in complete metamorphoses. Thus, for example in sequence, the egg, larva, pupa and adult may be shown in life like manner on the monitor, as these changes occur.

CAI is one mode of instruction which can meet the personal needs of students in mathematics. The styles of learning differ among learners in the classroom. Brief mention was made in this manuscript initially of the basal textbook method. The writer, in supervising university student teachers in the public schools, noticed many pupils who did well in mathematics using this method of learning. A well prepared and enthusiastic teacher can also do much to assist pupil achievement. Here, the class as a whole, committees, and individual study may be used to assist pupils to achieve objectives in mathematics. Audio-visual aids may be used in large group instruction to initiate and clarify major concepts and generalizations contained in the ensuing lesson, from the basal textbook. The basal stresses the scope and sequence of subject matter content to be emphasized in the curriculum. Within that framework, subject matter content is chosen for daily ensuing lessons. Generally, this follows the order of content presented in the basal. Which are relevant objectives of instruction in mathematics? The following, among others, are salient for pupils to attain in ongoing lessons and units of study:

- knowledge of symbols, formulas, graphs and operations on number.
- number systems, place value and key structural ideas.
- meaning of essential content in plane and solid geometry.
- rational and logical thinking.
- critical and creative thinking.
- problem solving and project methods of learning (See National Council Teachers of Mathematics, 2006).

Both inductive and deductive methods may also be used. There can be considerable flexibility in methods used when the basal textbook serves as a guide in teaching mathematics. A teacher's manual accompanying the basal provides a listing of objectives for each lesson, learning activities to achieve objectives and evaluation procedures to notice student progress. Diagnosis of pupil errors may also be inherent in the manual.

In closing

Any approved approach in teaching mathematics must be based upon sound principles of teaching and learning. Pupil interest needs to be fostered in ongoing lessons and units of study. Learners should be actively involved in achieving well in the mathematics curriculum. Meaning and understanding must accrue when vital concepts and generalizations are acquired. Pupil purpose is salient to develop as well as maintain. Thus, there must be reasons for achieving sequential objectives. Individual differences need to be provided for, among pupils.

There are disadvantages in using either CAI or Basal mathematics textbooks in teaching mathematics. For example, CAI may hinder social development of pupils since interaction with computers, not people is involved. Basal textbook use may become boring with sequential pages followed each day in teaching. It is advantageous to vary the methods and procedures of instruction to secure the benefits of using any one approach in teaching mathematics.

Mathematics teachers need to be concerned about the attitudes and feelings of students. There needs to be quality communication among teachers and students. Respect for each person in the school and classroom setting is important. Patience should be shown when students learn necessary skills in working with computers. Also, there needs to be a thorough understanding of what motivates pupils to achieve. Motivation is a key concept in learning (See National Research Council 2001).

REFERENCES

Djeassilane, N. (2008), "Effect of Computer Aided Instruction (CAI) in Enhancing the Academic Achievement of Higher Secondary Students in Commerce. Ph D thesis evaluated by Marlow Ediger for Alagappa University, Karaikudi-630003, India.

Ediger, Marlow (2005), "Teaching Mathematics in the High School Setting," *College Student Journal*, 39 (4), 711-715.

Ediger, Marlow (2006) "Writing in the Mathematics Curriculum," *Journal of Instructional Psychology*, 33 (2), 120-123.

Ediger, Marlow and D. Bhaskara Rao (2001), *Teaching Mathematics Successfully*. New Delhi, India: Discovery Publishing House.

National Council Teachers of Mathematics (1989), *Curriculum and Evaluation Standards for School Mathematics*. Reston, Virginia: NCTM.

National Council Teachers of Mathematics (2006), *Curriculum Focal Points for Kindergarten Through Grade Eight Mathematics*: A *Quest for Coherence*. Reston, Va.: NCTM.

National Research Council (2001), *Adding It Up. Helping Children Learn Mathematics*. Washington, DC: National Academy Press.

Wiske, S. (2004), "Use Technology to dig for Meaning," *Educational Leadership*, 63(1), 478.

27 School Mathematics and the Pupil

Mathematics has long been considered as one of the three 'r's (reading, writing and (a)rithmetic) and is a basic in the curriculum. It has gone through a history of change. During Colonial America times, memorization, definitely was a major method of teaching. Teachers, generally, then had children memorize the basic addition addition, subtraction, multiplication, and division facts until they were mastered. Joseph Lancaster, in the early 1800s, developed a sequence in teaching the basic number facts with each of the following taught separately: simple addition, compound addition with carrying being involved, simple subtraction, compound subtraction with borrowing involvement, simple multiplication, compound multiplication, simple division, compound division. Each was taught separately, such as simple addition from simple subtraction. Shortly thereafter, the object lesson was brought into teaching situations using the methods of Johann Friedrich Pestalozzi (1746-1827). Thus when learning to add, pupils would count objects, for example, 3 objects + 2 objects made 7 objects, making learning more enjoyable as well as meaningful at the same time. Friedrich Froebel (1780-1852) also used the concrete for kindergartners. He designed special materials for teaching. These included spheres, cubes, rectangular blocks, model lines and points, as well as rings. His methods of teaching were highly informal. Emphasizing the use of mother play songs, Froebel stressed pupils being in a geometric circle while singing and creatively dramatizing the content in the song. He stressed the salience of the sphere as being the most poignant of geometric figures since it contained no edges. Mathematical ideas were stressed throughout his writings.

Recent Developments in Mathematics Instruction

Mathematics instruction received major impetus in 1958 following the Soviet Union launching the first satellite to encircle the planet earth in 1957. Thus, the National Defense Education Act (NDEA) was passed in the United States which emphasized "modem mathematics". Textbooks were revised to incorporate the philosophy of university mathematics instructors identifying key ideas and the structure of mathematics. The structure stressed the saliency of teachers assisting pupils in their respective classrooms to achieve these structural ideas inductively, thus working as professional mathematicians do in their professional endeavors. Many workshops were funded by NDEA moneys. Materials for teaching mathematics were greatly reduced in price, generally 50 per cent, when approved by the state department of education. There were scholarships for teachers to take university course work to upgrade mathematics teaching. There were even stipends for spouses and children when going along with the spouse to a university, removed from home base. This was indeed an outstanding time to improve the curriculum, especially in mathematics, science and foreign languages.

Compared to today, students obtain massive debts in attending college/university courses. Students then may accumulate $50,000 in debt after four years. Securing a teaching position may be difficult in times of recessions in the economic world. Those having teaching positions begin at approximately $45,000 beginning salary. This does not leave much leeway for living expenses and at the same time paying off debts. Tuition to attend an institution of higher learning varies, but costs approximately $1050 a semester hour. As an undergraduate and master's degree student, the writer paid $4.50

for each semester hour of credit in the 1950s when inflation was much less rampant. As compared to the 1950s, subsidizing education by the state is very lax as of this writing in September, 2012. One has to be very poor or brilliant to secure a scholarship. This makes it all the more important for pupils to be diligent in achievement in the public schools. Thus, in school and in society, high mathematics achievement is poignant!

A well-planned sequence in mathematics must be in evidence in the mathematics curriculum. Thus, mathematics objectives of instruction are based on the present achievement level of individual learners. Progress in mathematics then is based on pupil ability to attain the ensuing objective. This cannot not be hurried, nor should subject matter repeat what was acquired previously. However, the teacher needs to encourage each pupil to reach upward in attainment as much as possible. Scaffolding is important to utilize in instruction. Thus, a pupil can achieve more optimally with ordered questions asked by the teacher. In this way, scaffolding does assist learners to achieve at a higher rate of progress. Quality sequence does not frustrate achievement, but actually encourages more optimal progress.

Mathematics should be an enjoyable academic discipline. Too frequently, it is not liked by pupils. Mathematics teachers need to stimulate learning by:

- varying the kinds of materials used in teaching. Using the textbook only for instructional procedures may make for a lack of interest in learning. Utilization of concrete materials in instruction might well aid achievement if sequenced property. Thus, viewing models of circles and seeing how they are used in society encourages interest in finding the area of a circle. I see, for example, many circle drives and circular windows on buildings. Then too, understanding why the formula "pi times radius square" is utilized helps pupils to perceive relationships of 3.14 times the radius squared. Thus, there are 3.14 squares in each circle. Relationships are of utmost importance to emphasize.

- meaningful subject matter is salient to emphasize. Pupils need to understand content, not memorize for testing purposes only/largely.
- motivating pupils to achieve rather than forcing learning. Too frequently, covering much ground in pages covered in a basal textbook rather than truly developing feelings of inner energy for attaining objectives of instruction is stressed. There is a great difference in attempting to assist learners in becoming motivated individuals rather than commanding forced learning to achieve predetermined objectives of instruction. Motivation from within does not depend upon tokens, prizes and parties for achievement in teaching and learning situations. Rather, pupils need to have an inward desire to learn in mathematics. Learning indepth with interesting experiences helps pupils to enjoy mathematics in an increasing manner.
- varying procedures utilized in the evaluation process. The following might be innovative procedures in the assessment process: using portfolio methods, doing a project and appraising its finality, dramatizing a mathematical situation, doing a drawing of a concept, collaborative evaluation of learner progress in a completed lesson, discussing, "What did we learn today," in an ongoing unit of study in mathematics.
- objectives, too, might well be varied. Thus, critical thinking may be stressed whereby in a collaborative situation, the small group may become engaged in problem solving. The problem might come from the basal textbook, the teacher, or learners themselves. Time and effort are involved here. The committee must analyze the problem in terms of what is wanted as a solution. If estimation is needed, learners may suggest ensuing hypotheses. These need evaluation with actual measurement, using appropriate tools to do the task. The hypothesis is either accepted, rejected, or modified.

For a change in objectives, learners might need to develop a generalization. Thus adequate information must be gleaned inductively to achieve the generalization. The secured information is subordinate to the generalization. Accuracy of separating the major ideas from those of lesser value must be evaluated. Pupils with teacher guidance may check their generalization by noticing carefully if each subordinate idea supports the major generalization. By weighing each main idea with that of supporting subordinate ideas, pupils at the appropriate developmental level may come up with a solid generalization. It takes time and effort for learners to become proficient in acquiring problem solving skills as well as achieving major generalizations. Effort is a key concept here.

There are times when pupils feel they cannot achieve well do to failure or failures experienced. It becomes difficult to "bounce back" from negative experiences. The mathematics teacher needs to assist pupils to continually develop a good self concept. Encouragement of the learner and stressing the importance of, "You can if you try," plus scaffolding, if necessary, aids pupils in attaining loftier goals. To achieve desired attitudes, the teacher must help learners in attaining quality attitudes which must be ongoing, in time, covering a plethora of mathematical units of study. "Recovering" from any negative experience, the pupil needs to realize that the latter happens to all, and all learn to recoup. Those who are successful individuals learn from past mistakes and modify, change their responses.

Ample subject matter knowledge, alone, is not adequate, there also needs to be teaching and learning skills in in implementing the curriculum. Mathematical knowledge must be put to use in various procedures including:

- everyday practical activities.
- computerized games.
- committee work and endeavors.
- basal mathematics textbook experiences.
- No Child Left Behind standards.
- Common Core State Standards.

Each pupil needs to achieve as optimally as possible. Learning activities must aid learners to attain objectives, as well as evaluation techniques used in assessing pupil achievement. Indepth teaching and learning is a definite trend to emphasize.

REFERENCE

Ediger, Marlow and D. Bhaskara Rao (2012), *Essays on Teaching Mathematics*. New Delhi, India: Discovery Publishing House (Ltd.).

Trends in Teaching Mathematics

Mathematics teachers need to study trends in the curriculum to notice what needs to be changed/modified in teaching and learning situations. Individually or cooperatively, studying trends in mathematics instruction aids in upgrading the curriculum. This tends to minimize the gap between *what is* and *what should be* in guiding optimal achievement in learners. Which trends are salient to emphasize?

Innovation in the Mathematics Curriculum

1. The scope and sequence of each unit need to be carefully designed. Scope stresses *what* should be taught. The totality of knowledge, skills and attitudinal objectives should be addressed here. Rational balance among these three kinds of objectives is important. New objectives may need to be added and a few modified or changed to meet current trends. Clarity in writing objectives is a must! Determining the scope of the mathematics curriculum emphasizes indepth understanding of what comprises a quality mathematics curriculum for learners.

Sequence stresses *when* specific facts, concepts, and generalizations are to be taught. Each new objective to be emphasized in teaching needs to be based on previous learnings acquired. Relating the new with the old provides for readiness in achievement. Subject matter should not be taught in isolation, but as being related. This aids not only in achievement, but also in retention due to one idea triggering another. Thus, the order of mathematical experiences for pupils assists in securing more optimal attainment (Ediger and Rao, 2007).

2. Metacognition is an important concept to stress in teaching. Here, the teacher guides pupils to reflect upon what has been learned. The pupil then rehearses what has been achieved as well as realizes what is left to learn. The learner, too, reflects upon that which lacks clarity. Self diagnosis and remediation is involved. Vagueness in understanding and achieving objectives may then be corrected through teaching and learning as in the following:

- regrouping and renaming in one of the four basic operations of addition, multiplication, subtraction, or division.
- negative numbers and their use.
- changing fractions to decimals.
- finding the per cent of a number (Ediger, 2007).

3. The psychology of learning must permeate the instructional arena. This assists pupils to achieve objectives more readily and effectively. Psychological tenets and principles of learning need to be stressed in any lesson and unit of study. To do so can truly make for quality teaching and learning situations. The mathematics teacher must study and analyze diverse psychologies and try out different schools of thought in the classroom. The following are agreed upon principles of instruction:

- pupils need to be fully engaged in learning to optimize teaching and learning situations. Thus, learning activities must be interesting in order to attain objectives of instruction.
- pupils need to attach meaning to each process taught in ongoing lessons. They may become hindered in achieving if previously taught content was not understood. Readiness factors indicate a need for the learner to build upon acquired facts, concepts and generalizations in mathematics.

- pupils need to perceive purpose in learning. Thus, the learner perceives reasons for finding the area or circumference of a circle. To show how the subject matter is used aids the pupil in sensing a need to learn. Motivation to learn is then emphasized in ongoing lessons and units of study (See National Council Teachers of Mathematics, 1989).

4. Grouping pupils for instruction helps to individualize instruction. The mathematics teacher needs to study pupil progress carefully to notice how to group for instruction. Homogeneously grouped pupils are of similar achievement levels. Heterogeneous grouping stresses mixed achievement levels of learners. Pupils may also be grouped according to interests possessed in mathematics. The teacher then must place each pupil in the group which optimizes accomplishment. For example, the mathematics teacher groups selected pupils homogeneously since learners here are challenged by solving complex word problems. They are of similar ability levels. In an interest group, learners achieve more, here, due to like interests in doing a project such as developing a glossary on recently studied geometrical terms. Pupils are fascinated in working on most projects.

Large group instruction stresses teaching those learnings which all pupils need and achieve in this kind of setting. Small group instruction individualizes and elaborates on that discussed and presented in a large group session. Vygotsky (1978) was a strong advocate of small group or committee endeavors. He believed that learning occurred in social situations whereby participants interact with each other. Ideas then "bounce off the minds" of individuals and learning occurs within the group discussion. Problem solving in mathematics should work well in these kinds of situations. Criteria must be set up so that positive behavior is inherent. Rudeness and derogatory remarks hinder achievement among learners. Individualized activities, as a third kind of experience, provide opportunities for the pupil to pursue a task from the mathematics learning center which provides enrichment and purpose.

5. Resilience in learning is salient. Here, the pupil is able to rebound successfully from being unsuccessful. The teacher must provide activities which are on the developmental level of learners and provide for success. Success tends to motivate and activate pupils to achieve more complex ordered learnings. However, situations occur, in all of life, where a lack of success is experienced. Thus with encouragement and appropriate learning activities, the pupil is able to develop feelings of success with resilience being an end result. Resilience is a marvelous trait in which the pupil is again ready to pursue a new objective. Not giving up is important! The teacher or a peer may well be able to provide the incentive to keep working and trying. There is much to learn in the mathematics curriculum and each day presents opportunities to attain, accomplish, and master subject matter as well as needed skills (Ediger, 2008).

6. A positive self-concept is necessary for pupils to feel they *can* achieve mathematical objectives in a favorable way. Adequate background information provides readiness for tackling a new process or procedure in an ongoing lesson. An advance organizer may be used as a teaching strategy to introduce a mathematical unit which involves the teacher providing an overview of what will be studied by pupils. Concrete (objects and items), semi-concrete (illustrations, diagrams, picture charts, video tapes, dramatizations, and computerized programs), as well as abstract (mathematics basal textbooks, quality supplementary work books and work sheets, as well as computer programs), might well be used as learning activities and in teaching strategies to provide for individual differences in the classroom (See Myers, 2008).

Support systems, too, help pupils to feel more positive when experiencing difficulties in attempting to achieve objectives. Thus, there is assistance from the teacher, teacher aid, and/or peers when help is needed in a given situation. The assistance is provided in a positive manner with no ridiculing or rude remarks. Then too, pupils like to hear praise for work well done. Each pupil may receive praise if his/her achievement has improved over previous performances. The self concept then provides confidence within the learner to attain more complex learnings. Pupils need to possess feelings of belonging and acceptance in the classroom, as well as have esteem needs met.

7. Mathematics teachers need to grow and develop in teaching skills and knowledge in a sequential manner. Through inservice education, mathematics teachers develop confidence that they can and do teach well to meet a variety of classroom needs of pupils. English Language learners (ELL), the mentally retarded, and the gifted, among others, can be assisted to achieve as optimally as possible. Inservice education may consist of workshops, faculty meetings, taking online and on campus course work, research projects and reading recent literature on teaching mathematics from the school's professional library assists teachers to develop confidence to do a good job in teaching pupils (See Wiske, 2004).

In Closing

Teachers of mathematics need to study recent trends in teaching pupils. These trends may be tried out in the classroom and modified, if need be. The important point is to provide for individual differences in the classroom and assist each pupil to optimize achievement.

REFERENCES

Ediger, Marlow (2007), "Readiness for Mathematics Learning and the Student," *Experiments in Education*, 35 (8), 1-5.

Ediger, Marlow (2008), "Modern School Mathematics," *College Student Journal*, 42 (4), 986-989.

Ediger, Marlow and Digumarti Bhaskara Rao (2007), School Science Education. New Delhi, India: Discovery Publishing House.

Myers, Perla (2008), "Why? Why? Why? Future Teachers Discover Mathematics in Depth," *Phi Delta Kappan*, 88 (9), 696.

National Council Teachers of Mathematics (1989), *Curriculum and Evaluation Standards for School Mathematics*. Reston, Va: NCTM.

Vygotsky, Len (1978), *Mind in Society: The Development of Higher Psychological Processes*. Cambridge, Massachusetts: Harvard University Press.

Wiske, S. (2004), "Using Technology to Dig Deep for Meaning," *Educational Leadership*, 62 (1) 8.

29 Problems in Teaching Mathematics

The mathematics teacher must have—through knowledge and skill in teaching and learning situations. He/she must also under-stand the approximate developmental level of the child in order to provide a strategy which engages the learner to achieve vital objectives of instruction. Pupils differ from each other in many ways and these need to be considered in planning for instruction. For example, they reveal differences in mathematical intelligence and ability. These talents need nurturing, while other abilities, too, must be attained as optimally as possible. In a competitive society, pupils need to become proficient in mathematics for use in school and in society (Ediger, 2008).

Seven Problems in Guiding Pupil Achievement and Progress

1. Pupils must be challenged in ongoing learning opportunities. The objectives to be achieved need to infer high expectations from the teacher and yet each objective is attainable. Effort must be forth by the learner to develop, grow and achieve. Encouragement needs to be in the offing. Scaffolding as a method of teaching stresses that the pupil's "proximal zone of development" makes it possible to move from where he/she is presently in achievement and then attain a selected higher ideal of accomplishment. Through teaching cues and use of appropriate materials of instruction, the pupil can achieve the otherwise too complex objective of instruction. Scaffolding

then emphasizes assisting pupils from their present state of achievement to a challenging new level of attainment. That difference from what is to what is desired stresses scaffolding. The teacher's role is to ascertain where each pupil is now in achievement as compared to where the desired level at which the pupil should be. It is not easy to do this. It requires judgment, knowledge and skill of the teacher (Vygotsky, 1978).

2. The mathematics teacher must provide for individual differences among learners. Thus, the math teacher needs to possess adequate knowledge of individual pupil achievement. Selected pupils will be quite independent in achievement of objectives. Others will need more assistance. In providing for individual differences in the classroom, the teacher needs to:

- achieve a wide repertoire of teaching skills.
- managing mathematics classes effectively.
- design a meaningful mathematics curriculum.
- feel motivated to sequentially improve pupil achievement.
- read articles on improving teaching and learning situations (Ediger and Rao 2001).

3. Selected pupils might need help in reading word problems. The mathematics teacher needs to be a teacher of reading in order to provide help where decoding words is involved in achieving objectives. Thus, he/she may read aloud, while struggling pupils in reading follow along in their basal mathematics textbooks. In this way, pupils may be aided in understanding what has been read rather than being frustrated and hindered in comprehension. Assistance in word recognition/comprehension may also be given in the following ways:

- helping learners to use context clues.
- guiding pupils to use cues such as initial consonants and their related sounds to recognize unknown words.
- using picture clues to recognize an unknown word. Thus if a pupils gets stuck on a word, he/she may see

if an illustration on that age gives away the unknown word.

- dividing an unknown word into syllables to notice if this aids in recognizing the unknown.
- looking for a smaller known word inside of the longer unknown word (Ediger, 2006a,b).

4. The teacher must have a good knowledge of mathematics in order to help pupils attach meaning to what is not understood. To frequently, teachers lack indepth knowledge of mathematics to guide pupils who fail to attach meaning to what is being taught. If pupils fail to understand, the teacher must use relevant knowledge to assist pupils in goal attainment. A different algorism, a new teaching aid used such as a place value chart, a fraction chart used to teach equivalent fractions, among other vital procedures, assist pupils in achieving objectives. The math teacher needs to stay abreast of current knowledge and methodology to help pupils attain as optimally as possible (See Kennedy and Tipps, 1991).

5. Quality attitudes arise as a result of interacting with learning activities in the math curriculum. Strategies in teaching need to provide for success in attaining challenging objectives. The learner needs to feel he/she can and does achieve. With metacognition, the pupil reflects upon what was accomplished specifically in ongoing lessons and units of study. With reflection, the pupil reviews and rehearses. He/she also realizes gaps in knowledge and skills which need to be remedied in teaching and learning. Self-diagnosis stresses that remedial work may need to be emphasized.

Good attitudes toward mathematics help in wanting to learn more subject matter. If high quality attitudes prevail, the chances are the learner will be as successful as abilities permit. However, the pupil must always reach out, feel inward challenge and compete against the self to optimize achievement (Ediger, 2006).

6. Continuous inservice education is a must! Teaching becomes increasingly motivated when the teacher feels he/

she is a professional in mathematics instruction. There are different ways to foster growth, development and progress as a teacher:

- quality workshops in which participants apply in the classroom that which was presented. Participants might then provide feedback on how the innovative approach worked in teaching and learning situations. The results are discussed and, perhaps, result in additional innovations.
- internet courses which emphasize teaching mathematics. These online courses are given by accredited colleges and universities. Both content and methodology are being stressed.
- classes taken on accredited, higher education campuses. These provide opportunities for acquiring subject matter, as well as methods of teaching.
- attendance at local, state and national conferences in teaching of mathematics.
- an independent study taken which involves research on teaching and learning. A variety of reference sources are used which focuses on high quality research methodology.
- seminars developed which encourage local mathematics teachers and professors discussing the implementation of recent trends in teaching.
- grade level meetings to look at innovative ideas used in teaching.
- faculty meetings involving discussing mentoring in the classroom(See National Council Teachers of Mathematics, 1989).

7. Parent/teacher conferences are important to discuss the offspring's progress in mathematics achievement. Different facets of pupil progress need analyzing with recommen-dations made to facilitate learning. Parents and the school must work cooperatively to solve problems. By working together, the involved pupil should have assurance

that his/her achievement does matter to significant others. A portfolio can be an excellent way for the child to communicate to the teacher and parent what has been done to achieve objectives of instruction. The learner may then pinpoint from the portfolio, for example, what has been accomplished in mathematics on selected days (See Peressini, 1997).

In Conclusion Throughout the mathematics curriculum, the teacher must stress critical and creative thinking, as well as problem solving. These skills are relevant now as well as in society. They are salient in school as well as at the future work place.

REFERENCES

Ediger, Marlow (2006a), "Scaffolding and the Reading Curriculum," *Iowa Educational Leadership*, 8 (4), 24-26.

Ediger, Marlow (2006b), "Writing in the Mathematics Curriculum," *Journal of Instructional Psychology*, 33 (1), 120-123.

Ediger, Marlow (2008), "Modern School Mathematics," *College Student Journal*, 42 (4), 986-989.

Ediger, Marlow and Digumarti Bhaskara Rao (2001), *Teaching Mathematics Successfully*. New Delhi, India: Discovery Publishing House.

Kennedy, Leonard M. and Steve Tipps (1991), *Guiding Children's Learning of Mathematics*. Belmont, California: Wadsworth Publishing Company.

National Council Teachers of Mathematics (1989), *Curriculum and Evaluation Standards for School Mathematics*. Reston, Virginia: NCTM.

Peressini, D. (1997), "Parental Reform of Mathematics Education," *The Mathematics Teacher*, 90 (6), 423-427.

Vygotsky, Len (1978), *Mind in Society: The Development of Higher Psychological Process*. Cambridge, Massachusetts: Harvard University Press.

Quality Teaching in Mathematics

The best teaching possible needs to accrue in the mathematics curriculum. Pupils also need to become proficient in using mathematics in every day situations in life. Individuals buy goods and services. They pay for these in different ways, including cash. Here, persons need to be able to compute the total cost of items purchased and then pay for them using adequate currency amounts.

In the school setting, much use is made of number such as how many pupils will eat in the cafeteria at noon or how many want milk in the school milk program? There are, indeed, a plethora of situations involving the use of mathematics. What might the teacher then do to assist pupils to develop proficiency in numeracy and use mathematics effectively in school and in society?

Teaching and Learning in Mathematics

A major problem in teaching is that the teacher may wish to move forward too rapidly within a lesson which makes for pupil difficulty in keeping up with the facts, concepts and generalizations being taught. The mathematics teacher must pace lessons whereby pupils may be successful in mastering the content presented. If the pacing is too rapid, pupils may not attach meaning to what is being taught. Toward the other end of the continuum, if the pacing is too slow, boredom may set in. The teacher must observe pupils carefully while teaching to notice if there is understanding of subject matter being taught (Ediger and Rao, 2002).

There needs to be adequate pupil interaction with content being taught. The mathematics teacher may then be more certain that each pupil does attach meaning to ensuing content. For example, the teacher may observe pupils, at their desks, if they can show the meaning of regrouping by taking a set of fourteen sticks and placing them into a set of ten with four remaining. The resulting number may be shown in the semi-concrete, such as 14 sticks being equal to one ten and four ones on a place value chart. Numerous markers may be used to show meaning, as well as hands on approaches to learning. Active involvement of learners is better than being passive recipients, according to research findings (Ediger, 2008).

Interaction among pupils needs to be encouraged. Thus, ideas may circulate among pupils when cooperative endeavors are used in problem solving. Pupils then contribute in problem solving situations and build on the thinking of others. Ideas and contributions must be respected and politeness must be inherent in the discussion. This aids in more input from learners. A relaxed environment for cooperative endeavors encourages thinking. Vygotsky (1978) stressed the importance of small group work in which ideas "bounce of the heads" of learners. He also emphasized the concept of *scaffolding* in teaching and learning situations. Thus, if a pupil does not understand a complex concept in mathematics and yet it is achievable. The teacher may sequence with concrete and semi-concrete learning activities, in small steps, which then leads the learner to the initial complex concept in the abstract.

Learners need to develop connections in ongoing lessons and units of study. They need to learn, for example, the connectedness of $5 \times 4 = 4 \times 5$. Thus, selected structural ideas become salient such as the commutative and associative properties of multiplication and addition as well as the inverse operation of addition and subtraction and multiplication and division. Also, pupils need to connect the mathematics curriculum with the self in solving personal problems. Then too, mathematical problems as they relate to society must find solutions. The learner does not live unto an island by the self, but is interrelated to and with others (Ediger, 2006).

Pupils need encouragement to be creative in finding their own best way to solve problems. There are different algorithms to use in finding answers to many problems. Mathematics teachers may present models here as well as support pupils who do venture out with novel ideas for solutions. Creativity is useful presently for learners as well as for the future in the societal arena. Innovations and progress have come about due to creative ideas being stressed (See National Council Teachers of Mathematics, 1989).

Making estimations in terms of answers to problems is salient for pupils. It is practical to be able to make quality estimations such as in distances and in costs of items purchased. This takes knowledge and skills which are built up sequentially. In all situations in teaching mathematics, pupils need to experience interesting activities to achieve vital objectives of instruction. They need to perceive purpose or reasons for acquiring important knowledge and skills.

A rich mathematics vocabulary must be developed to perform diverse algorithms as well as to communicate mathematical ideas. The vocabulary terms must have meaning to be used effectively in contextual situations (See Burns, 2007).

A professional mathematics teacher needs to possess pedagogical content knowledge and includes:

- what ideas about or understanding of a concept students are likely to have before instruction.
- typical difficulties students tend to have in learning a given concept or topic.
- what order to introduce concepts and skills to minimize confusion about a topic.
- what strategies work to help different kinds of students overcome common difficulties.

- how to choose and use instructional materials.
- what models/analogies/visualizations/activities work well to convey specific understandings.
- how to assess what students have learned about a given topic (Jeyanthi, 2008:43-44).

It is very important for the mathematics teacher to understand mathematical knowledge and skills possessed by pupils. A pretest and direct observation of each pupil's achievement will provide much information in terms of what the starting point should be in teaching an ensuing lesson or unit of study. From that point on, the teacher may design a curriculum based on developmental needs of pupils. Diagnosis of learning difficulties, too, must be analyzed. Remediation efforts may then follow. The mathematics teacher might well teach in a way that sequential learnings accrue. The mathematics teacher must continually observe individual pupils to notice what kinds of assistance are necessary to provide for optimal pupil achievement and progress. Sequential presentations of salient concepts and generalizations are needed to provide strategies which assist pupils to make continual progress. Inductive, deductive, multi-media, problem solving and/or tutorials, among others, may be used to help pupils overcome difficulties and achieve (See Wiske, 2004).

To teach effectively, the mathematics teacher needs to be well versed in subject matter content. He/she must explain facts, concepts, and procedures clearly and in an appropriate order. Indepth understanding needs to be developed by learners. Math teachers need to be well prepared in knowledge to be able to explain what is vague or unclear to pupils. An effective teacher foresees content problems which pupils might experience. He/she also has the indepth knowledge to ascertain which facts, concepts and generalizations to teach so that meaningful learnings accrue to pupils. Analogies may need to be used to clarify ideas for pupils. Thus, in context, the teacher may use examples through drawings, diagrams, and illustrations to show mathematical ideas to learners. Demonstrating the use of subject matter must be in proper order, developmentally appropriate, challenging and assist in achieving successful learners. Knowledge of mathematics must not be separated from processes and procedures of teaching. The goal of integrating knowledge of mathematics with pedagogy is to assist pupils in attaining sequential objectives (See Peressini, 1997).

Attitudinal Development

The teacher serves as a role model for pupils in developing a quality attitude toward mathematics. The successful teacher possesses teaching efficacy. Self-efficacy is developed by the teacher in building upon previous foundations of cumulative mathematical knowledge and skills attained as well as on successful years of teaching experience. The efficacious teacher becomes confident in teaching pupils who come from various backgrounds and persuasions. These attitudes then are passed on to pupils. A positive attitude toward mathematics and toward teaching math is salient. Pupils feel this attitude coming from the teacher and it becomes a part of the repertoire of learners in the classroom. Jeyanthi (2008: 47) lists the following characteristics of attitude:

- attitudes are evaluative and can be presented on some continuum of favorableness.
- attitudes vary in intensity and direction.
- some attitudes are accompanied by or connected with a person's emotions.
- attitudes are relatively durable.
- attitudes are learned and can therefore be taught.
- attitudes are related to behavior.

Quality attitudes in teaching mathematics then is of utmost importance. The teacher presents a role model for pupil emulation. Good attitudes can be learned by pupils. Greater achievement in mathematics is possible for all learners.

REFERENCES

Ediger, Marlow (2006), "Writing in the Mathematics Curriculum," *Journal of Instructional Psychology*, 33 (2),120-123.

Ediger, Marlow (2008), "Modern School Mathematics," *College Student Journal*, 42 (4), 986-989.

Ediger, Marlow, and D. Bhaskara Rao (2001), *Teaching Mathematics Successfully*. New Delhi, India: Discovery Publishing House.

Burns, Marilyn (2007), "Nine Ways to Catch Kids Up," *Educational Leadership*, 65 (3), 16-21.

Jeyanthi, S. (2008), Cognitive and Attitudinal Correlates of Teaching Performance of B.Ed., Mathematics Students. Ph D these evaluated by Marlow Ediger for Mother Teresa Women's University, Kodaikanal, India, 43-44 and 47.

National Council Teachers of Mathematics (1989), *Curriculum and Evaluation Standards for School Mathematics*. Reston, Va.: NCTM.

Peressini, D. (1997), "Parental Reform of Mathematics Education," *The Mathematics Teacher*, 423-427.

Vygotsky, L. S. (1978), *Mind in Society: the Development of Higher Psychological Processes*. Cambridge, Massachusetts: Harvard University Press.

Wiske, S. (2004), "Use Technology to dig for Meaning," *Educational Leadership*, 62(1), 478.

31 Meaning in the Social Studies

An important factor in teaching social studies is to develop meaningful learnings for pupils. Thus, pupils must understand what is taught. Through a variety of developmentally appropriate activities, pupils may attach meaning to relevant facts, concepts, and generalizations, as well as skills. They should help pupils to attain vital objectives of instruction. With valid and reliable means of evaluation, social studies teachers may ascertain if pupils have been successful achievers. Quality principles of learning must be . used in teaching to guide more optimal pupil achievement and progress.

Meaning, the Pupil and the Social Studies

When assisting pupils in reading social studies subject matter, teacher first must assist pupils to possess adequate background knowledge. The background knowledge relates directly to the ensuing content to be read. Relating the new content to that previously acquired, helps pupils to perceive the relationship of knowledge. Meaningful learnings then accrue. By looking at the illustrations in the basal, pupils may be motivated to predict what *will be* in the new content. These predictions may be checked with subject matter acquired after the content has been read (Ediger and Rao, 2000).

In addition to providing background information for reading the ensuing subject matter, the teacher also needs to assist pupils with recognizing new words to be met in print.

The new words may be printed on the chalkboard or via computer and magnified on the screen. Each of these words needs to be used in sentences as they appear in the basal. Thus, familiarity with word identification will enable a pupil to recognize each new word as the ensuing reading activity progresses. As a followup experience, pupils with teacher guidance may use the subject matter read in:

- developing an experience chart, summarizing major conclusions from a discussion.
- making models from paper mache' or molding, moist paper towels.
- doing a continuing classroom book on content learned from sequential social studies units of study.
- taking a teacher and/or pupil made test to evaluate comprehension.
- placing new words on a classroom word wall (Ediger, 2008).

Technology might well take an equally important role as do traditional methods of having pupils read subject matter. This may especially be helpful to pupils with reading difficulties. Thus, electronic texts need to be in the offing in the social studies. With computer and software use, pupils may experience the following:

- the subject matter read aloud while pupils follow along with the printed script on the monitor.
- music and animation to go along with the contents.
- new words pronounced. Words and definitions, or within contextual sentences, may be provided by the computer with a click of the mouse.
- computer technology can do away with problems of word recognition and the necessity to wait for assistance from a busy social studies teacher.
- tests from the computer may assess learner progress. Test results are stored by the computer to notice

specific kinds of pupil errors for diagnostic purposes and for learner progress in achievement (See Rhodes and Milby, 2007).

When readiness is in evidence, pupils may also be guided to achieve higher levels of cognition. This includes critical thinking in separating facts from opinions, fantasy from reality, and accurate from inaccurate information. Creative thinking, too, might well be emphasized. Here, pupils are challenged to come up with new, unique ideas. Novel ideas are needed in society which can make for innovations in school and in society. Critical and creative thinking are necessary to solve environmental problems, offer solutions to settle disputes between and among individuals and nations, as well as to use resources wisely. The following problems, also, need solutions within a state or nation:

- what to do about the national debt.
- solving the housing/mortgage crises.
- how to tax people equitably.
- emphasis upon more full employment.
- solving disagreements within and outside a nation through diplomatic channels.
- saving the environment and natural resources, including much attention paid to global warming (See, National Council for the Social Studies, 1994).

The above are key problems in the natural and social world. Lessons and units might well be built around these identified problem areas. A good current events program should aid pupils in making intelligent decisions. Knowledge objectives are important, but so are skills ends including analytic, synthetic, and evaluative objectives. Facts, alone are not adequate, but higher levels of cognition are needed in a quality current events program. Meaningful learnings are salient. Traditional methods as well as computerized approaches may be used in guiding pupils to higher cognitive levels of thought.

Monitoring, Reflecting and Metacognition

When pupils read or participate in other learning activities, they should learn to monitor their own individual progress. Here, the pupil, when reading for example, will continually notice if comprehension is taking place and not word calling only. When reading is done, the reader wants to understand that which is read. Too frequently, a pupil is reading social studies subject matter, but fails to attach meaning to ideas being read. The same may be said about participating in discussions, the pupil must understand its contents or time is being wasted. By monitoring, the pupil assesses ongoing comprehension. Then too, the pupil needs to reflect upon content read or discussed. When reflection is taking place, the pupil rehearses and analyzes subject matter from content read or discussed. Review is taking place and this helps the learner to retain ideas. Use is made of previously acquired subject matter.

Metacognition pertains to "thinking about thinking." Thus, the pupil looks back at facts, concepts and generalizations acquired as well as skills achieved to ascertain their completeness. The pupil then notices:

- subject matter lacking meaning.
- ideas which lack clarity.
- weaknesses in plans pertaining to a problem solving activity or a project which is in progress or completed.
- processes used in a discussion.
- improvements and refinements necessary in computer usage (See Noddings, 2008).

Monitoring then has to do with evaluating if one is currently understanding sequential ideas within a learning activity. Reflecting deals with assessing content read or discussed, just recently. Metacognition emphasizes thinking about ideas and skills having been studied to ascertain what needs further elaboration.

Inservice Education

Social studies teachers must continually grow and develop professionally in teaching and learning. A professional library for teachers must be available in school, housing the latest in educational journals as well as teacher education textbooks. The internet must be accessible to teachers to view the latest in state and national journals in teaching social studies. Grade level meetings of social studies need to be encouraged whereby ideas may be shared. Workshops for social studies teachers need careful planning with vital topics being pursued. Teachers need to have opportunities to try out innovative ideas from the workshop in their own individual classrooms and report back to workshop members the success of the teaching endeavor (Sawchuk, September 10, 2008).

More inservice education opportunities are available to teachers than ever before. Online education makes it so that teachers may work at their own suitable time with no driving to distant places. Thus, inservice education may be done right in the home of the teacher. There are excellent online courses designed for social studies teachers. The times are indeed convenient for course taking. These need to meet personal teaching needs. Many accredited universities offer online graduate teacher education classes. Coursework also may be taken on a university campus leading to a graduate degree. Social studies teachers need to stay abreast of recent trends in teaching and learning. The psychology of teaching social studies needs to be given full attention such as engaging learners in each lesson and unit of study, pupils attaching meaning to ongoing activities as well as perceiving purpose in learning. From social science coursework, social studies teachers need to acquire structural ideas pertaining to each of the following academic disciplines useful in the preparation of lessons and units of study:

- history with relevant ideas dealing with the past. Primary sources are important to integrate into the curriculum.
- geography as it relates to place location and how these relate to interaction with other regions.

- political science with its emphasis upon laws, rules and regulations and their affect upon human beings.
- economics including concepts such as goods, services, consumption, production, distribution, opportunity costs as well as advantages
- culture (anthropology and sociology) with the study of human inventions and institutions and their affect upon human behavior (See Parker, 2001).

Each of the above need indepth study, analysis, meaning, and elaboration to improve teacher knowledge and skills in teaching the social studies. Quality attitudes should result toward the social studies curriculum and pupil achievement. Interest in computer use and technology is a motivating factor in staying abreast of what is current in teaching the social studies.

In Conclusion

A Position Statement of the National Council for the Social Studies (2008) states the following pertaining to a "Vision of Powerful Teaching and Learning in the Social Studies":

- Key concepts and themes are developed in depth. The most effective social studies teachers do not diffuse their efforts by covering too many topics superficially. Breadth is important, but deep and thoughtful understanding is essential to prepare students for the issues of twenty-first century citizenship.
- Skills necessary to help our students thrive in a world of continuous and accelerated change are emphasized. These include discipline based literacy, multicultural awareness, information gathering and analysis, inquiry and critical thinking, communication, data analysis, and the prudent use of 21st century media and technology. Skills are embedded throughout meaningful social studies lessons, rather than added on at the end.
- Teachers are reflective in planning, implementing, and assessing meaningful curriculum. Reflective teachers

are well informed about the nature and purposes of social studies, have a continual, growing understanding of the disciplines that they teach and keep up with pedagogical developments in the field of social studies.

- Meaningful curriculum includes extensive and reflective study of the United States and other nations' histories, religions and cultures.

REFERENCES

Ediger, Marlow (2008), "Reading in the Social Studies," *Florida Council Social Studies eNewsletter*, pp. 1-3.

Ediger, Marlow and D. Bhaskara Rao (2000) *Teaching Social Studies Successfully*. New Delhi, India: Discovery Publishing House.

National Council for the Social Studies (1994), *Curriculum Standards for the Social Studies*, Washington, DC: NCSS.

National Council for the Social Studies (2008), A Vision of Powerful Teaching and Learning in the Social Studies; Building Effective Citizens," *Social Education*, 72 (5), 277-278.

Noddings, Nel (2008), "All Our Students Thinking," *Educational Leadership*, 65(5), 8-13.

Parker, Walter C. (2001), *Social Studies in Elementary Education*. Merrill, Prentice-Hall: Upper Saddle River, New Jersey.

Rhodes, Joan A. and Tammy M. Milby (2007), "Teacher Created Electronic Books: Integrating Technology to Support Readers With Disabilities," *The Reading Teacher*, 61 (3), 255-259.

Sawchuk, Sean (September 10, 2008), Leadership Gap Seen in Post-NCLB Changes in U.S. Teachers," *Education Week*, 28 (3), 1,16.

The Changing Social Studies Curriculum

The social studies curriculum changes and is modified to meet demands of pupils in the 21st century. Memorization of subject matter leaves much to be desired and is very limited in use in society. Rather higher levels of thinking are necessary to function well in school and in the societal setting.

The Modern Social Studies

Social studies units of study must be chosen carefully. There is much that is desired from the public schools, social studies achievement being no exception. Thus, each objective must contribute to developing a contributing member of society. Which are these knowledge, skills and attitudes that need to become objectives of instruction? The Middle Ages will be referred to frequently in the ensuing discussion.

A first criterion to be discussed in an updated social studies program involves analytical thinking. To analyze is to separate needed from unnecessary content, for example, in problem solving. Thus, a problem area is identified such as, "How did farming accrue on a manor during the Middle Ages?" Using diverse reference sources on the developmental level of learners, pupils may come up with concepts such as crop rotation, horses pulling a wooden plow, serfs, slaves, flails, castle, huts, church, among others. These must be connected to secure an hypothesis to the chosen problem area. The internet provides selected excellent illustrations related to the concept. Thus, meaning may be attached to each abstract concept. Comparisons may be made with farming of today with self propelled combines and air conditioned cabs including hydraulic lifts to raise or lower the cutting level for grain. Tractors, also with air conditioned cabs, use hydraulic lifts and are used for pulling implements to plow, disc and seed crops. During 1940s draft horses were no longer used to pull farm implements, but many farmers had hand cranks to start a tractor when no starter was available. Self-propelled combines were rapidly coming into being to harvest grain crops. Manual labor has been greatly minimized in farming. Hay balers used following windrows of cut alfalfa make large 1000 pound bales automatically which at a later time are taken by tractor, with a hydraulic lift, to where cattle are fed. Cold/hot castles of the Middle Ages, depending upon the season, have been replaced with houses having centralized air conditioning for the different seasons of the year, depending upon hot/cold temperatures. Serfs and slaves have long been a thing of the past and there would, anyway, be no use for them presently due to technological uses on farms. Thus, there are a plethora of uses for critical thinking in the social studies with the above examples in separating the medieval days from present times in problem solving arenas. Second, creative thinking is a must in social studies units of study. Here, pupils need to come up with unique, novel ideas. Originality of thought needs to be tapped with learning activities which capture pupil imagination. Too frequently rote learning is stressed and this should be replaced with novel ideas. Thus, in the Middles Ages unit of study, learners might well be placed in an atmosphere of freedom of thought whereby the following, among others, may be an end result:

- brain storming a related project which needs to be completed.
- developing a model manor using a variety of media such as clay/play dough, construction paper of diverse colors, and cardboard, among others.
- role playing the work of a guild member in doing a selected type of work.

- planning and doing a reader's theater on a tournament of events held on a lord's manor or in life on a monastery.
- completing a mural of a church on a manor.
- doing poetry writing with rhyme such as a quatrain with four lines of ending words rhyming; a limerick with lines one, two and five rhyming as well as lines three and four having rhyme. Limericks, generally, begin with, "There once was..." Free verse, also, might be written with no designated rhyme or length. Verse with syllabication is fascinating for those who possess readiness; Haiku has lines one and three each having five syllables with line two possessing seven syllables. All of these poems are challenging to write and many find these interesting to complete.

Third, pupils need to learn to read pictoral content. There are numerous pictures in basal textbooks as well as in audio-visual aids which contain excellent illustrations of life in the Middle Ages. The three stages of becoming a knight shows the page who has just entered the study of knighthood with entry learnings in becoming a knight, the second stage of being labelled a squire who has learned the skills accruing in its duties and finally being "dubbed" a knight by a priest in a church where communion was being taken as well as fasting by the knight, the night prior to securing the actual title.

Reading illustrations/pictures breathes life into the unit being studied. Thus, pupils need to understand subject matter being studied. In addition, retention of leanings is aided with pupils using content acquired as in:

- writing diary entries in the life of a page who is just beginning the first stage of knighthood development.
- developing a bulletin board display on the medieval church.
- doing a research paper, using a variety of references, on the rank of "squire" in becoming a knight.
- reporting to the class summarizing knighthood acts when *tournaments* were held on a Lord's manor.

Fourth, quality reading and writing skills are essential for pupils to learn in the social studies. There are objectives which teachers need to have pupils attain in reading such as the following:

- identifying unknown words in context. These become identifiable as pupils choose a word for the unknown which fits into the rest of the sentence or paragraph. Sometimes, a pupil will substitute an outlandish choice for an unknown word and this fails to make sense pertaining to meaning in a contextual situation.
- using basic phonics to assist in word recognition. Thus, if a pupil fails to identify a word while reading, he/she is guided to look at the initial consonant and sound out that letter or combination of letters in the unknown. This procedure, along with the use of context clues, will provide the learner with the correct word in numerous situations.
- if the above named two approaches fail, then the teacher should orally pronounce the unknown so that the pupil does not loose the trend of thought.

Certain initial consonant sounds need to be taught, especially those which are relatively consistent between symbol and sound as in the letters b, d, f, h, k, l, m n, p, r, t. These can be taught as the need arises, not with long drills on sounds that are not relevant in time.

With a considerable amount of reading, the pupil notices sentence structure and how words are utilized in sentences. For initial writing experiences, young children may dictate social studies content observed such as items on an interest center, followed by the teacher using manuscript letters, for pupils to view, as the recorded words proceed in print. Pupils then notice that ideas may be recorded on paper or by using the word processor.

Sequentially, the teacher may guide pupils to become increasingly independent in writing with the *correlation* of the language arts in the use of:

- simple sentences containing a subject and predicate.
- adjectives to modify nouns as well as adverbs to modify verbs, adverbs and adjectives.
- compound sentences with adjective, adverb and noun subordinate clauses.

Each of the above should be taught in purposeful social studies writing activities and not as drill. Drill might be stressed in small degrees once pupils have revealed basic leanings on sentence structure. Drill should definitely not be used for punishment, nor in initial learnings. Rather, learner interest, enthusiasm and purpose is to be fostered in all learning. Accuracy in content written is salient, and experiences in creative writing do stress the imaginative and the unique (Ediger and Rao, 2011).

In summary

Pupils need to experience much critical thinking as in analyzing subject matter and in problem solving. Rote learning and memorization have long been outdated when emphasizing a stimulating environment which encourages optimal learner progress. The social studies has a long history of being important in the curriculum (Ediger and Rao, 2012).

Johann Friedrich Herbart (1776-1841), in what is now Germany, emphasized five sequential steps of learning in teaching pupils, consisting of preparation in reviewing what had been taught previously, presentation which stressed having pupils learn the ensuing content, association whereby learners relate what was contained in the steps of preparation and presentation, generalizations in which pupils developed a summary or conclusion, and finally use what has been acquired. Where did Herbart place the social studies in importance? He advocated two core academic areas, history and literature. With the recent 'No Child Left Behind' law of 2002, social studies was completely omitted in importance. Hopefully, the Common Core State Standards will reverse this trend as well as teachers, on their own, strongly emphasizing the social studies in the curriculum.

REFERENCES

Ediger, Marlow and D. Bhaskara Rao (2011), *Essays on Curriculum Development*. New Delhi, India; Discovery Publishing House (Ltd.).

Ediger, Marlow and D. Bhaskara Rao (2012), *Essays Teaching Social Studies*. New Delhi, India: Discovery Publishing House (Ltd.).

Needed Modifications in the Social Studies

The Social Studies must experience change in order to provide useful learnings in school and in society.

The changes are necessary in order to better prepare individuals for a changing society in a technological world. There are selected knowledge, skills and attitudes which learners need to be fully functioning persons in a world of change.

Change and the Social Studies

Pupils need to develop skills in problem solving. Situations in life emphasize individuals continually selecting and attempting to find necessary solutions. There are problems, for example, which indeed are difficult to determine solutions such as in the Middle East dilemma between Jews of Israel versus the Palestinian Arabs in the land formerly called Palestine. Both want the same area of land of which Israel is in definite control presently.

The changing social studies must keep up with changes in borders between and among nations. The following are changes in borders in Palestine:

- Israel declared statehood in 1948 involving 80 per cent while the nation of Jordan had 20 per cent including the West Bank.
- Israel captured the rest of Palestine in the 1967 Six Day war which involved Jordan, resulting in a plethora of Arab refugees. Egypt and Syria fought with Jordan in

this war. Israel also captured the Sinai peninsula from Egypt as well as the Gaza Strip. In addition, Israel in the Six Day War of 1967, captured the Golan Heights from Syria. It remains to be seen who will be the victor in the present civil war in 2012 between the present government of Syria and the rebels.

- Israel annexed the walled city of Jerusalem and built settlements on the West Bank which now totals 500,000 Jews. Israel also has 25,000 settlers on the Golan Heights.
- the Sinai was returned to Egypt in 1978 with a signed peace treaty between Israel and Egypt. With the overthrow of the Egyptian government in 2011, it remains to be seen what will happen to the Egyptian/ Israeli Treaty.
- the Gaza Strip was captured and then settled, in part, by settlers from Israel, but due to hostilities between Arabs and Jews was vacated in 2001. Gaza is ten by twenty miles in dimension and is inhabited and governed by the Palestinian Arabs.

There is much need for pupils to engage in map/globe studies showing the land of Palestine before 1948 when Great Britain had the Mandate to govern this land. In sequence, learners must study and analyze the land of Palestine when Israel became a nation in 1948 and the West Bank became a part of the nation of Jordan. Changes in context should be noted on these maps/globes when Israel captured the rest of the West Bank from Jordan in 1967. The following cities on the West Bank, in particular, must receive attention in terms of their saliency on the West Bank:

- The walled city of Jerusalem containing the Western Wall, the only remnant of the ancient Jewish Temple. This is the holiest place on earth for the Jews of Israel; the Dome of the Rock, an octagonal Mosque built in AD 691; and the church of the Holy Sepulcher, originally bullet in AD 330 and refurbished in 1099 when the Crusaders captured the Holy Land.
- Bethlehem, five miles south of Jerusalem, the home of the Church of the Nativity, where according to devout

Christians Christ was born. Inside this Church is the Grotto area which King Constantine and his mother Queen Wilhelmina, in AD 330, identified as the exact spot of Christ's birth exemplified by a fourteen point silver star.

- Hebron, the city containing the Mosque of Abraham, also called the Tomb of the Prophets, Inside this structure are the Tombs of Abraham and Sarah, Isaac and Rebecca, as well as Jacob and Lean; these are the Patriarchs and their wives of ancient Israel and also considered prophets by the Islamic religion.
- Samaria, also named Nablus, and is located 45 kilometers north Jerusalem, houses the Tomb of Joseph, a son of the Patriarch Jacob. Going upward on Mount Gerizim in Nablus is the compound and home of the Samaritans. The Samaritans are the result of the intermarriage of the ancient Israelites and the Assyrians who captured and deported men of the Kingdom of Israel in AD 732.

To achieve the objectives above, pupils need to study and read illustrations of the Western Wall, the Dome of the Rock, as well as the Church of the Holy Sepulcher. Indepth discussions might well lead to understanding major historical events on each of these well known structures. Meaning and understanding are salient in teaching and learning situations. Thus, the Church of the Holy Sepulcher is very closely related to the Crusades, AD 1099-1187 in which the Crusaders captured the walled city of Jerusalem and took over the Church until AD 1187. Problems arise which need solutions involving studying ancient history such as:

- Why is the Western Wall holy to devout Jews of Israel?
- What importance is the Dome of the Rock to Muslims?
- Why is it salient to analyze Samaritan culture such as those on Mount Gerizim?
- How is the Church of the Nativity significant to followers of Christianity?

A variety of reference sources must be utilized to acquire data and information for each of these identified problem areas. Pupils may work individually or collaboratively in ongoing learning experiences involving problem solving. Technological use and textbook, workbooks, newsmagazines, as well as daily newspapers, might well assist in determining solutions to problem areas (Ediger and Rao, 2011).

Current Problems in the Holy Land

The two state solution of a separate state of Palestine or the Arabs alongside of Israel has been a traditional proposal for bringing some kind of stability to the conflict between Arabs and Jews. However, this possibility appears very remote as Israel builds more settlements on the West Bank, which formerly, before 1967, was Arab in population. Presently 500,000 Israelis have settled on what was formerly Palestinian land. The walled city of Jerusalem has been modified with almost complete Israeli control. When serving with MCC on the West BAnk being a part of Jordan, one could travel rather freely to different cities in this area and also into what is presently the nation of Jordan. Presently, a tall wall was built to separate the walled city and its environment from the rest of the West Bank. Cars are inspected thoroughly by Israeli police when traveling from Jerusalem, for instance, to Bethlehem, a distance of five/six miles.

Refugees are always a problem in war situations. In the present civil War in Syria, approximately 500,000 refugees have fled to neighboring Jordan. When fighting was going on in neighboring Iraq, approximately 800,000 Iraqis also fled into Jordan. Wars make for refugees but also for a plethora of deaths, lost arms and legs, brain damage, and post traumatic stress syndrome. Creative statesmen and women are needed to solve problems among and between nations, without the use of crater and concussion bombs as well as bombs in general, self propelled rocket grenades and troops on the ground.

REFERENCE

Ediger, Marlow and D. Bhaskara Rao (2011), *Essays on Teaching Social Studies*. New Delhi, India: Discovery Publishing House (Ltd.).

Constructivism and the Social Studies

Constructivism, a psychology of learning, has its many adherents in social studies teaching. The student is central in the teaching and learning process. The teacher assists, guides, and encourages student progress. He/she does not lecture, nor lean upon giving students lengthy explanations of subject matter content. Inductive learning by the student is strongly stressed in ongoing lessons and units of study. Social studies textbooks may be used as one avenue of learning, but there are a plethora of other reference sources to be used in a multi-media curriculum (Ediger, 2007).

Basic Guidelines to Emphasize in Constructivism Constructivism stresses that students personally interpret facts, concepts and generalizations. Students attach meaning to what has been learned and the knowledge acquired is subject to modification as well as revisions as new concepts and generalizations are achieved. Problem solving, as an example, stresses the importance of constructivism. Within an ongoing social studies unit, the student identifies a question which personally needs to be answered. The question must be clearly stated. An hypothesis is developed which is a temporary solution, acquired by using a variety of reference sources.

The hypothesis is evaluated by securing content from different reference sources such as the internet, basal social studies textbooks, encyclopedias, library books and knowledgeable persons, among others. If needed, the hypothesis is refuted, changed, or modified. New problems might well arise within a problem solving experience. Constructivism emphasizes that students change perceptions as engagement in learning accrues. It is the student who is actively involved in learning; the teacher is a resource person to assist and help. As the student's knowledge and skills increase, he/she changes perceptions and comes up with a more holistic set of concepts and generalizations. Thus, subject matter knowledge and abilities evolve into a new perspective (Parker, 2001).

Project methods in teaching social studies emphasize that students work individually or collectively in achieving objectives in an ongoing unit of study. The ideas for the project come from learners themselves with teacher assistance. Purposes are accepted by the involved students in developing the project. Careful planning of the project is salient. Implementation of the plans requires neat, meticulous work in realizing completion. Criteria developed by the students with teacher guidance are needed to appraise the quality of the project. A hands on approach in learning is emphasized in doing projects. If a collective endeavor is involved in doing the project, appraising the contributions of each member is important in terms of effort put forth as well as good workmanship. Projects decided upon and completed may include the following:

- developing a personal portfolio containing a representative sampling of written products such as book reports, essays, a digital picture brochure/folder of completed work, among others.
- a bulletin board, a mural and a word wall containing relevant vocabulary terms encountered in the ongoing unit of study.
- an indepth journal kept on relevant social studies activities and learnings.
- a model made such as of a bedouin village in a desert region.

- an accurate relief map showing major cities and sea ports, mountainous areas, plains, plateaus, among other geographical representations. A quality legend needs to accompany the relief map (see National Council for the Social Studies, 1997).

The focus in solving a problem and on doing a project is upon the learner who is actively engaged in decision making. Decisions made are based upon possessing necessary background information and meanings attached to the ongoing learning activity in the social studies. Interest is important in motivating a student to pursue and achieve worthwhile learnings. Learners must have time to reflect upon what has been accomplished within an experience such as in problem solving or in doing relevant projects. Readiness factors are inherent when cognition is involved in an activity centered social studies curriculum. Going from the known to the unknown is salient in a constructivist psychology of learning. The student is not a passive being but is fully involved in the ongoing lesson/unit of study (Ediger, 2008).

Attitudes and feelings are important in constuctivism. Students learn to care, share and help each other. With the use of learning centers in the classroom, for example, students may choose experiences whereby group work is involved. Thus, a classroom may have four or five centers, each having five tasks to choose from sequentially. Tasks may be omitted which lack perceived purpose. Teacher/pupil planning may also be stressed in choosing learning opportunities. One task might stress peer learning whereby a social studies library book is chosen to read and discuss. Here, standards are involved in which each participant is actively participating, but not dominating the discussion. Respect for each participant and his/her ideas is emphasized. Learners assist each other in constructing meaning and understanding content read. Rudeness, dogmatism and dictating ideas within the peer setting are definitely frowned upon. Each participant builds upon previously developed content (See Dunn, 2008).

The peer discussion might well lead to a related, challenging followup experience such as:

- debating an issue identified in the reading activity.
- dramatizing key economic concepts such as goods, services, an assembly line, inflation, recession/depression, credit cards, loans, interest, leveraged buyouts, mortgages, and payments.
- making a series of charts such as showing the organization of state and of federal government; developing a vocabulary chart with accompanying illustrations; among other possibilities (Ediger, 2007).

Helping students to achieve well stresses the importance of learners doing well intellectually, socially, emotionally and physically. The whole child is involved with changes occurring as he/she perceives knowledge as being subjective. Precise, measurable results of student progress are not possible due to maturation. Jean Piaget who for fifty years studied child development in Geneva, Switzerland came up with the following stages of pupil development in the maturation process:

- sensori-motor, ages birth to two years of age.
- preoperational, ages two to seven years.
- concrete operations, seven to eleven years of age.
- abstract thought, ages eleven and on up in sequential growth (Imholder and Piaget, 1958).

Tremendous changes occur in a pupil's life from birth to the abstract stage whereby the latter can think largely/completely in the abstract when reading and discussing ideas in the social studies. Constructivist theory is based upon changes in pupil development and how things are perceived in life as scenes and situations change.

Constructivism Versus Behaviorism

Behaviorism stresses a thoroughly predetermined social studies curriculum with objectives stated prior to instruction. The objectives are generally stated in measurable terms so that a student either does/does not achieve each objective. No leeway is left to plan objectives with learners. Learning activities to achieve objectives are chosen by the teacher and they are aligned with the objectives. Success in social studies achievement is based upon the number of objectives achieved.

Mandated testing generally emphasizes the use of multiple choice test items. Answers then are marked either right or wrong by students. Machine scoring can check answers in large volumes in tests given to many students with results provided in precise numerical terms such as in percentiles or grade equivalents. This provides feedback to teachers on how well each student has done in social studies achievement. The feedback may be used for teacher accountability as well as for diagnostic purposes. Each student's results may be compared with his/her previous test scores. There is no guess work in ascertaining student progress with behaviorism used as a means of instruction. (Guilfoyle, 2006). Behaviorism stresses:

- data driven decision-making. Test scores, as results, are used to notice student progress and for decision making purposes in instruction.
- assumptions pertaining to objectivity in selecting objectives for instruction, aligned learning opportunities and precise numerical results of students from testing.
- measurement results from students are wanted, not subjective interpretations of learner achievement.
- student progress might then be plotted on a line or bar graph to notice progress.

Cognitive objectives receive primary emphasis in teaching pupils with standardization stressed in the curriculum including the following in testing situations:

- the test items are the same for all pupils on a given grade level.
- the directions given for test taking are the same.
- the scoring key is the same for all tests on a specific grade level.

In conclusion

There are major differences when making comparisons between a constructivist versus a curriculum emphasizing behaviorism. These differences include the following:

- constructivism is more open-ended to student input into the curriculum. Thus, the learner is central in the teaching and learning situation whereas in behaviorism, the teacher selects objectives, aligned learning activities, and appraisal procedures to ascertain if the precise ends have been attained.
- constructivism stresses the use of teacher observation, along with learner self evaluation, to notice pupil progress. Behaviorism emphasizes using tests to ascertain pupil achievement; numerical results from testing are important to behaviorists.
- constructivists stress that sequence resides within the pupil whereas behaviorists emphasize predetermined teacher or mandated objectives, properly ordered, to determine sequence in teaching.

REFERENCES

Dunn, Ross E. (2008), "The Two World Histories," *Social Education*, 72 (5), 257-263.

Ediger, Marlow (2002), "Current Events in the Social Studies," Edutracks, 7(3), 14-15.

Ediger, Marlow (2007), "Meaning in Reading Instruction," *Reading Improvement*, 44 (4), 217-20.

Ediger, Marlow (2008), "The Old Order Amish and the Social Studies," *Viewpoints*, 38 (4), 13-16.

Guilfoyle, Christy (2006), "NCLB: Is there Life Beyond Testing?" *Educational Leadership*, 64 (3), 8-13.

Imholder, Barbel and Jean Piaget (1958), *The Growth of Logical Thinking From Childhood to Adolescent*. New York: Basic Books.

National Council for the Social Studies (1997), *Curriculum Standards for the Social Studies*. Edison, New York: Whitehurst and Clark.

Parker, Walter C. Parker (2001), *Social Studies in Elementary Education*. Upper Saddle River, New Jersey: Merrill, Prentice-Hall.

Sequence in the Social Studies

Quality Sequence in the Social Studies is of Utmost Importance. Sequence Emphasizes "When" Selected Concepts Shuld be Stressed in Ongoing Lessons and Units of Study. The social studies teacher needs to observe pupils carefully in teaching and learning situations to ascertain suitable, ordered experiences for pupils. Pupils face frustration if the learning opportunities are too complex and may feel boredom if the tasks are too easy. Carefully sequenced facts, concepts and generalizations assist pupils to attain more optimally, be it in programmed learning or in open ended approaches. What might the social studies teacher do to assist pupils achieve more optimally in the social studies? (Ediger and Rao, 2002)

Diverse Plans in Determining Sequence in the Social Studies

Programmed learning stresses that the programmer determines objectives, learning activities and evaluation procedures, in a particular order. The learning activities are very closely aligned with the objectives and move from the simple to the complex in a tightly planned sequence. Pupils make few mistakes in a pilot studied, published program. Thus, for example, a pupil at a computer terminal, reads a few sentences, then responds to a multiple choice test item, covering what has been read. He/she immediately receives an answer of being either correct/incorrect. If incorrect, the pupil sees the correct answer on the monitor and is also ready for the next sequential learning. This sequence of read, respond and check is followed continuously. Each learning builds on the previously sequential subject matter content acquired by pupils. By carefully sequencing information from one step of learning to the next, the pupil experiences much sequential success. The emphasis here is upon responding correctly, which *reinforces* each step of learning. Operant conditioning is then in evidence. The late B. F. Skinner was a leading exponent of programmed learning and operant conditioning (Ediger and Rao 2003).

Teaching toward mandated objectives is more open ended as compared to operant conditioning, but it still stresses the teacher focusing upon closure in terms of pupils achieving what is measurable. Pupils, here, take annual tests containing multiple choice test items. The test items are aligned with precise or specific objectives of instruction. This has made it that teachers attempt to teach toward the specific objectives only, so that pupils score higher on the mandated, required tests. The scope of the curriculum is delimited to that which is tested. Sequence in teaching then pertains to the order of objectives pupils are to attain. Measurable test results are emphasized in the use of programmed learning as well as in the mandated objectives curriculum (Ediger, 2007).

Toward the other end of the continuum are problem solving methods, quite popular today, in teaching the social studies. Problem solving is rather open ended in that within an ongoing lesson/unit of study, pupils choose a problem to solve. The problem is salient and requires effort and deliberation in its solving. A variety of references are used to gather necessary information. They include the internet, basal social studies textbooks, encyclopedia entries, library books and knowledgeable personnel, among others. The information is organized to be used in securing an answer to the problem. The answer, here, becomes a tentative hypothesis to be tested. If the tentative answer holds up under scrutiny due to critical and creative thinking, then it is accepted. If not, the original hypothesis is modified or refuted. Problem solving is flexible, and is sequenced by learners with teacher guidance. John Dewey (1859-1953) was a leading advocate of problem solving (Dewey, 1916).

The project method is closely related to problem solving approaches and stresses that pupils, also, largely sequence their own work in ongoing social studies units of study. Here, within an ongoing unit of study, pupils choose a project to develop with teacher assistance. The project generally stresses a small group endeavor which tends to emphasize a construction activity. The activity has relevance to the involved learners and possesses a perceived purpose to these pupils. The project then is not emphasized for the sake of doing so, but rather to fulfil a need. Carefully planning is necessary and stresses cooperation among pupils. The plans are carried out with modifications as needed. The final product is then appraised in terms of desired criteria. A project activity approach in learning is highly pupil centered with sequence residing within the learner as he/she works within the group to plan, develop, and evaluate the purposeful project (See Sharma and Sharma, 2009).

Constructivism in teaching the social studies emphasizes that pupils create their own knowledge as a lesson or unit progresses. With enriched experiences, the pupil gains knowledge to develop more comprehensive concepts and generalizations. There are no absolutes, the pupil continues to achieve, grow and develop in a stimulating social studies environment. The teacher is a guide and helper of pupil progress, not one who lectures or has precise predetermined objectives stated prior to teaching for learner attainment. With constructivism, learning is ongoing and cannot be measured, but through teacher observation assistance is given as needed to motivate and encourage learning. Motivation comes from within the pupil as he/she sequences achievement in the social studies (See Parker, 2001).

Problem solving, project methods, and constructivism do not emphasize measurable results from pupil learning. Objectives, here, are not predetermined and stressed prior to teaching and learning situations. The doing part is sequenced by the learner with teacher guidance. Basal textbook methodology comes between behaviorism (programmed learning/mandated objectives philosophy of instruction) and action centered curricula (problem solving, project methods, and constructivism). A well and carefully chosen basal social studies textbook may be used as presented in the accompanying manual or modified to meet personal needs of pupils. Thus, the manual contains objectives for pupil attainment, learning opportunities to achieve the objectives, as well as evaluation procedures to provide feedback to teachers on pupil progress. Generally, social studies teachers feel the subject matter contained in each unit of study in the textbook needs extension and elaboration. The subject matter may come from the internet, reputable encyclopedias, library books, excursions, informed persons and AV aids, among other sources (See Association for Supervision and Curriculum Development, 2007). The basal textbook then:

- contains a structure with related ideas in designing and teaching the ongoing social studies unit.
- provides opportunities to clarify and amplify subject matter content.
- emphasizes a revised sequence to aid more optimal learner achievement.

Students should be challenged to raise questions pertaining to subject matter studied from the basal. These questions may well lead to searching for indepth information leading to critical and creative thinking.

When reading subject matter from the basal, the teacher needs to provide assistance in word recognition and comprehension of ideas. The following word recognition techniques should be stressed as needed:

- context clues to identify unknown words.
- phonics to use as clues to unlock new words.
- syllabication skills such as noticing root words, prefixes and suffixes and thus identify the unknown word.

- noticing short words within the larger word to aid and identify the unfamiliar (See Baumann, *et al.*, 2007).

Subject matter needs to be read with appropriate stress, pitch, and enunciation to avoid monotony and read with enthusiasm! Social studies can be an enjoyable academic area to study when:

- the content is related to the personal lives of pupils.
- pupils relate content studied to other people, nations, regions, and continents in the world.

The above named relationships aid pupils in attaining quality sequence, especially when relating it to their own personal lives. This makes the study of the social studies meaningful indeed! The personal talents and abilities, too, may be brought into each social studies unit as it enriches sequential learnings. The following talents, as examples, might well then be integrated:

- artistic to show scenes and situations being studied, such as well known persons in history, using a variety of art media.
- verbal as in reading and reporting on library books such studying people of other cultures.
- analytical, synthesis, objective and logical thinking skills in organizing and forming ideas.
- collaborative skills in working with other learners in an ongoing activity.
- manual dexterity to show abilities within concrete experiences.
- technology skills to gather subject matter from a variety of electronic sources.
- mathematical talents in measuring and doing construction work related directly to an ongoing unit of study (See Gardner, 1993).

Conclusion

Social studies teachers need to study learners in diverse kinds of situations to ascertain the best way to emphasize quality sequence in learning. Sequence stresses "when" is the optimal time to engage pupils in ensuing learnings. New learnings should not be too complex, nor too easy, but at a level which is challenging and yet the ensuing objectives are achievable.

REFERENCES

Association for Supervision and Curriculum Development (2007), *Education Update*, 49 (3), 1, 8.

Baugmann, James R, *et al.*, (2007), "Bumping Into Spicy, Tasty Words That Catch Your Tongue: A Formative Experiment on Vocabulary Instruction," *The Reading Teacher*, 61 (2), 108-124.

Dewey, John (1916) *Democracy and Education*. New York: Macmillan Publishing Company.

Ediger, Marlow (2007), "Learning Activities in the Curriculum," *College Student Journal*, 41 (4), 967-969.

Ediger, Marlow and Digumarti Bhaskara Rao (2002) *Teaching Social Studies Successfully*. New Delhi, India: Discovery Publishing House.

Ediger, Marlow and Digumarti Bhaskara Rao (2003), *Psychology and Curriculum*. New Delhi, India: Discovery Publishing House.

Gardner, Howard (1993), *Multiple Intelligences: Theory Into Practice*. New York: Basic Books.

Parker, Walter C. (2001), Social Studies in Elementary Education. Upper Saddle River, New Jersey: Prentice-Hall, Inc.

Sharma, Mala and Suman Sharma (2009), "Attitude of Science Teachers Toward the Project Method," *Edutracks*, 8 (6), 40-43.

Reading Comprehension in the Social Studies

Being able to read well is vital in the social studies. It is a valuable way of learning from the social sciences which provide content for the social studies curriculum. Pupils then need to become proficient in reading. Reading consists of word recognition as well as comprehension of ideas. Both must be stressed adequately in assisting the pupil to become a good reader in the social studies. This does not mean that the social studies becomes a reading course, but rather it facilitates the learning process in achieving relevant ideas. Subject matter learnings should facilitate the pupil becoming a knowledgeable, good citizen in society. Quality attitudes, too, are then acquired when pupils achieve relevant objectives of instruction (Ediger and Rao, 2002).

Readiness for Reading

An important consideration in assisting pupils to read social studies content is that needed prerequisites have been emphasized. Thus, pupils need to possess adequate background information. Building background information within pupils prior reading in an ensuing lesson helps the pupil to relate the new with what was previously learned. This also guides pupils to relate the new content to the self. Thus, the ensuing lesson must make sense to the involved learner. Background information may be provided by looking at illustrations on the same page as the scripted ideas to be read in the basal social studies textbook. Additional experiences in providing background information pertains to using a related videotape which clarifies subject matter content (See National Council for Geographic Education, 1994).

Readiness activities also stress pupils seeing the new words in print, prior to reading. These may be printed on the white board, use of the overhead projector, or on a screen with the enlarged words, through computer use. Pupils may then practice saying the printed words aloud, as well as using them in sentences.

A last readiness item is for pupils to identify questions they would like answered from the reading experience. Answers may be discussed as a followup. Indepth discussions might well lead to using a variety of reference sources to secure additional information. Branching out and extending learnings is to be welcomed, especially with involved pupil interests (See Roy, 2009).

Word Recognition in the Social Studies

Which word recognition techniques are salient for pupils to master? This depends upon the needs of pupils and which might also mean that there are common word recognition needs for all to attain. Word recognition should be taught in context, if at all possible. Problems in word recognition are then fresh in the minds of learners. If a pupil in a unit titled "The Middle Ages" is not identifying the word "guild in print," his/her attention should be drawn to the beginning letter "g" to notice its related sound which may either be the soft or hard "g" sound. Sometimes, the basal provides a phonetic spelling for the possible unknown word like "gild," not the soft "g" sound as in "jild." It may become necessary to immediately pronounce the correct word to a pupil so he/she does not lose meaning in ideas read. For a word such as "manor," the letter "m" has a highly consistent sound. Here, a pupil may benefit much from using phonics with the consistency between symbol and sound. There are familiar words which begin with the "m" sound and are familiar to lerners. Then too, the word 'manor' has a shorter word contained therein as in "man." There are a plethora of words ending in "or" with which pupils are familiar such as "tailor" and "favor." The pupil might then put together "man" and the "or" ending to make "manor." Both words (guild and manor), along with others, may be placed on a word wall in the classroom for future reference (Ediger, 2007).

Use of context clues are the best means for a reader to use in identifying the unknown. Thus, the pupil may be reading, "The (unknown word) lived on a manor." If the pupil notices the letter "s" and tries diverse words which fit in with the rest of the words in the sentence and paragraph, the chances are he/she will come up with the word "serf." Then too, "serf" is spelled quite consisntly phonetically. The "er" sound is familiar in many words such as baker, barber. Noblemen, slaves, serfs, knights and journeyman are words associated with the Middle Ages. These words may be added to the word wall as they are met in print by the learner. Pupils need to relate their lives in society with present day farmers being related in duties in life on a manor, knighthood to soldiering and the military, and guilds to manufacturing of products such as shoes, blankets, silver trays, dishes, among others. Guild members also provided services such as being a barber or meat cutter (See Reilly, 2008).

If pupils are struggling readers in the social studies, the basal text print may be enlarged by an opaque projector, with selected content reflected on a large screen. All pupils being taught, here, in a small group need to see the words clearly and pay careful attention as the teacher reads the content aloud as he/she points to each word. This may be repeated with pupils joining the read aloud.Thus, pupils may read the ensuing ideas without stumbling on individual words and thus lose interest in the subject matter. The writer when supervising university student teachers has noticed the following in pupils reading from the basal as supervised by the student teacher and the cooperating teacher:

- teachers reading aloud salient passages to a few struggling readers as the latter follow along in the basal textbook.
- pupils following along in their textbooks as an accompanying DVD plays the scripted ideas. Electronic aids are making the act of reading more suitable to the individual's present reading level.
- teachers scaffolding print for children. Thus with scaffolding, a pupil may understand more complex ideas as compared to what is printed. Intervening ideas may be presented to bridge subject matter extending that which exists in print, compared to an ideal envisioned by the teacher in teaching the social studies.
- a good reader reading aloud selected content to others who need assistance. Those receiving the assistance need to look at each word carefully as it is being read.

To promote interest in reading, the teacher needs to display relevant social studies library books and talk briefly about a few books to whet pupil attitudes for reading. Pupils individually then choose their very own library books to read. These might be read during the pupil's spare time or be taken home for reading. If read during a pupil's spare time, the social studies teacher may ask the learner a few relevant questions covering the content to notice comprehension as well as interest in reading. There are teachers who devote fifteen to thirty minutes a day in sustained silent reading (SSR). During this time, children may learn much social studies content on history, geography, sociology/anthropology, economics and political science. As a pupil in grade and high school, the writer enjoyed free time fir choosing self selected reading materials. If the pupil can choose social studies library books to read during spare time in school as well as in the home setting, reading skills and knowledge about the social studies should increase dramatically (See Cellano and Neuman, 2008).

Parent-Teacher Conferences

Parent-teacher conferences should include how well a learner is doing in knowledge, skills and attitudinal acquisition. Growth in knowledge objectives in the social studies should include the following:

* how well a child is achieving major facts, concepts and generalizations in ongoing units of study.
* how much time is devoted to reading library books pertaining to the social studies.
* how much effort is put forth in understanding main ideas.

The above-named asterisked items may be subdivided such as in concepts developed. In any unit of study, there are vital concepts to attach meaning to, as in the Middle Ages. Thus concepts such as the following may bridge the gap between the past and the present:

- methods of farming used.
- occupations, then and now.
- means of transportation, contrasting the Middle Ages with the present.

Skills objectives may be broken down into categories of demonstrated improvement in sequence, as well as that which needs further emphasis. Then too, specific learner needs in reading social studies subject matter may be analyzed into component parts with evaluation of pupil achievement each facet being important. Thus, the following may be analyzed in terms of pupil progress:

- use of context clues to identify unknown words.
- looks for smaller words within a longer word to identify the unknown.
- develops skills in phonic use to recognize the unknown word.
- understands what is being read.
- is able to summarize orally or in writing what has been read silently.

Attitudinal objectives which are salient to achieve include the following:

- reads social studies library books for enjoyment.
- has good attitudes toward reading from the basal.
- wants to identify unknown words.
- has an inward desire to read increasingly complex ideas (Ediger, 2008).

In Closing

Reading is a very important way of learning in the social studies. Other methods, too, need to be stressed in ongoing units of study such as the following:

- power point presentations and video-tapes related to ongoing units of study.
- DVDs, CDs, podcasts, and internet sources.
- knowledgeable resource personnel.

Thus, a multi-media approach should assist pupils to achieve more optimally.

REFERENCES

Cellano, Donna and Susan B. Neuman (2008), "When Schools Close, the Knowledge Gap Grows," *Phi Delta Kappan*, 94 (4), 256-262.

Ediger, Marlow (2007), "Meaning in Reading Instruction," *Reading Improvement*, 44 (4), 217-220.

Ediger, Marlow and Digumarti Bhaskara Rao (2002), *Teaching Social Studies Successfully*. New Delhi, India: Discovery Publishing House.

Ediger, Marlow (2008), "Leadership in the School Setting," *Education*, 129(1), 17-20.

National Council for Geographic Education (1994), *Geography for Life*. Washington, DC: NCGE.

Reilly, Mary Ann (2008), "Teaching the Right Words: Art Conversations and Poetry," *Language Arts*, 86 (2), 99-107).

Roy, Ruma (2009), "New Challenges in Teacher Education" *Edutracks*, 8 (6), 19-20.

Parent/Teacher Conferences in the Social Studies

Quality communication is needed between the parents and the school. Lines of communication need to be kept open. To often, there are hindrances to open communication due to time factors, inconsiderateness, rudeness, and haste. If pupils are to do well in school, there needs to be feelings that parent/teacher conferences are important. Too frequently, social studies is minimized or eliminated from communication time with parents. Traditional beliefs remain that the three r's (reading, writing, and arithmetic) are the only basics in the curriculum, but that indeed has narrowed the scope of the curriculum. Social studies has as a major objective to develop good citizenship which is so necessary in the global world. Accurate communication is important here, as well as in parent/teacher conference (Ediger and Rao, 2002).

Communicating Effectively

Which ingredients make for having ideas move freely from a sender to a receiver? Certainly, there are impediments to quality communication. These need to be removed or minimized as much as possible. Pleasant manners with an accompanying speaking voice which indicates consideration for others is salient. The manners incorporate non-verbal communication and need to be analyzed. Do they attract or repel others? Nervous gestures and facial expressions might well hinder effective communication. Teachers in a school need to see models of effective non-verbal as well as those which are ineffective on video-tape. Committees of teachers then need to discuss the "why" for each. Studying exemplars of quality parent/teacher conferences from appropriate reference sources in educational journals and teacher education textbooks provide guidelines for the ongoing discussion (Ediger, 2009).

It might be worth the expenditure to have consultant come in to assist with inservice education in conducting parent/teacher conferences. Roles may be played of the teacher and of the parent in the simulated environment. Problem areas are then identified and solutions sought. Involved problems include what kinds of information the teacher wishes Jp convey to parents such as pupil information on economic concepts Within an ongoing unit of study:

- goods, services, mortgages, liens, foreclosures, indebtedness.
- credit cards, interest, toxic loans, lender, borrower.
- payments, ATM machines, finance managing.

Sharing of ideas needs much stress during a parent/teacher conference. The concerns of parents require careful listening by the teacher in order that these may addressed. Perhaps, the parent is concerned about the lack of friends of the involved child. A framework might well be agreed upon to assist in friendship building. The child needs to be placed into a small group which is highly accepting of others in a social studies unit. A major concern of the teacher might emphasize that the child become a better listener. With the home and the school working together, solutions must be found to address problems identified during a parent/teacher conference. Then too, problems may be addressed at any time during the school year through:

- e-mail. The e-mail may be sent during a teacher's convenient time. Communication may occur as frequently as desired.
- telephone calls, either land line or cellular. The call may even deal with congratulating a child for doing well

on a social studies project. Voice recorders are handy when either the parent or the teacher cannot come to the phone at the time of calling.

- faxing messages in terms of necessary communication items, between home and school too, is becoming increasingly common.

There are numerous formal opportunities for parents to come to school and visit with involved teachers. These include:

- open house whereby samples of pupil work in the social studies may be displayed for the parent to view.
- parent/teacher organizations in which the former has an opportunity to visit with the social studies teacher (See Parker, 2001).

Quality communication between home and school is necessary in order to work together to provide the best learnings possible in the social studies. The objectives, learning activities to achieve the chosen ends and the evaluation procedures, need to be clarified and made meaningful to parents. The latter has an inward desire, generally, to assist their offspring to attain optimally. There is much the home can do to foster better achievement among offspring. At a very young age, the parent needs to read orally to the child using appropriate enunciation. Reading aloud with proper stress, pitch and juncture provides a model to the young child in learning to love social studies library books. The duration of the read aloud should not exceed the intrinsic interests of the young learner. The latter will have a short, attention span which needs to be adhered to. With older pupils, the parent and the learner need to engage in reciprocal reading whereby each reads a portion of the library book in sequence. Questions raised need to be discussed and meaning established. Pupils learn much social studies content by reading carefully selected library books. The library books should deal with a variety of genera and appropriate reading levels of the involved pupil (Kennedy, 2007).

Within the framework of parent/teacher conferences, much emphasis needs to be placed upon what both the home and the school can do to aid pupil progress. A follow through of the conference allows for evaluation in terms of its effectiveness. Additional ways the home and school can work together are the following:

- set up a plan, cooperatively, to assist pupils, for example, to improve in oral communication. Specific goals must be set with accompanying learning opportunities.
- determine ways to motivate pupil learning in the home setting, such as rewarding pupils for "*x*" number of library books read.
- take pupils on short excursions in the neighborhood to see salient sites, such as a museum. Discuss with pupils observations made.
- assist pupils to write up observations made, such as the excursion taken which is named above.
- make models of what has been read/studied in the home setting, such as a model parthenon pertaining to learnings on Greece.
- do a booklet on learning opportunities, experienced in the home setting. This provides excellent activities in using the internet and the word processor (See Dykstra, 2008).

The Portfolio in Communicating Achievement

A portfolio may be an excellent approach in evaluating pupil achievement in the social studies. Doing an electronic portfolio adds to the interests of doing things in the social studies. A portfolio developed by pupils with teacher assistance houses salient documents of pupil learning and progress. Thus, representative entries such as the following may be made in a social studies portfolio:

- summaries of book reports and other written work.
- outlines developed of salient subject matter.
- test results from teacher prepared tests.
- electronic photos of completed art work as well as construction projects and photo essays.

- recordings of reader's theater, oral reading and of creative dramatizations.

From the above, there are excellent possibilities for informal as well as formal parent/teacher conferences. In number one asterisk above, for example, parents may look at the quality of written work and progress made from one paper to the next. Significant facets to view in the evaluation process might well include the following:

- sequence of ideas expressed in written work.
- quality of spelling of words, including the use of spell checkers.
- agreement of subject and predicate.
- correct placement of modifiers.
- proper use of punctuation marks.

What is evaluated will depend, too, upon the developmental level of the pupil. There need to be high, but not unreasonable expectations for each pupil. Challenging goals need to be achievable. Based on the portfolio results, the parent and the social studies teacher need to agree upon several goals for the pupil to attain. At a subsequent conference, it can be noticed if these gaps have been eliminated (Ediger, 2007).

Report Cards to Report Pupil Progress

The traditional report card, issued every six weeks approximately, has some merits in its use. Together with other methods used to report pupil achievement, it might still be operational. The categories on the report card to convey pupil information on achievement may need to be modified. There are a plethora of questions which a parent may have as a result of viewing the report card, indicating six weeks in duration. Which are salient categories for reporting progress in the social studies? The following are a few which the writer has noticed on pupil report cards pertaining to all curriculum areas:

- puts for much effort in learning.

- perseveres in whatever is being studied.
- solves personal problems.*
- gets along well with others.
- works well with pupils in a committee setting (See Crawford, 2008).

Then there are other categories of evaluation pertaining to the social studies only, such as:

- reads library books and other social studies materials during spare time.
- likes social studies as a curriculum area.
- tends to work to his/her capacity in social studies achievement.
- volunteers to do extra work in ongoing lessons.
- writes on the social studies when a writing topic may be chosen.
- understands significant concepts in the social studies.
- develops a well made project for the annual social studies fair (a note might be attached to the report card pertaining to this yearly item).

Pertaining to the first asterisked item above, for example, a rating needs to be given on a five point scale. By looking at the ratings, the parent receives some idea as to how well the offspring is doing in each category. Areas of weakness need to be discussed with the parent and needed modifications made. If, for example, the child is weak in "likes social studies as a curriculum area," both the parent and the teacher need to brainstorm as to what might be done to change pupil behavior in this case (See Ryan, 2006).

REFERENCES

Crawford, Marilyn (2008), "Think Inside the Clock," *Phi Delta Kappan*, 90(4), 251-255.

Dykstra, Dee Vee E. (2008), "Integrating Critical Thinking and Memorandum Writing Into Course Curriculum Using the Internet as a Research Tool," *College Student Journal*, 42 (3), 920-929.

Ediger, Marlow (2009), "Scope in the Social Studies," *Edutracks*, 8 (6), 14-16.

Ediger, Marlow (2007), "Meaning in Reading Instruction," *Reading Improvement*, 44 (4), 217-220.

Ediger, Marlow and Digumarti Bhaskara Rao (2002), *Teaching Social Studies Successfully*. New Delhi, India: Discovery Publishing House.

Kennedy, Mary (2007), "From Teacher Quality to Teaching Quality," *Educational Leadership*, 63 (6), 14-19.

Parker, Walter (2001), *Social Studies in Elementary Education*. Upper Saddle River, New Jersey: The MacMillan Company.

Ryan, Tracey E. (2006), "Motivating Novice Students to Read Their Textbooks," *Journal of Instructional Psychology*, 33 (1), 135-140.

Recent Trends in Teaching the Social Studies

Teachers, Supervisors and School Administrators need to stay abreast of and implement selected trends in teaching the social studies. Pupils in classrooms then need to attain updated objectives of instruction, learning activities to achieve the objectives and evaluation procedures to analyze and notice pupil progress. The curriculum needs to be designed to reflect vital trends (See Fitzhugh, 2006).

Trends as Guidelines to Design the Social Studies

These trends provide for a viable curriculum when being studied and implemented. Careful analyzation is necessary in order for the teacher to attach meaning to and determine the worth of each trend. Which trends then are salient in the social studies?

First, pupils need to acquire relevant subject matter from the social sciences, which includes history (a study of vital main, subordinate ideas of the past and how they have influenced human beings), geography (the natural environment and its influence on human behavior), economics (purchasing and selling goods and services), political science (laws, rules, regulations and how they affect human beings) and anthropology/sociology (culture and its affect on human behavior). Key ideas and core concepts need identification and taught inductively as well as deductively, through explanations. These are incorporated into learning opportunities to assist pupils in attaining relevant objectives of instruction (See Parker, 2001).

Second, a multi-media approach must be used in teaching and learning situations in order to provide for individual differences. Concrete (actual items and objects), semi-concrete (illustrations, charts, drawings, picture library books, power point presentations, video-tapes, resource personnel, among others,) and abstract materials (textbooks, encyclopedias, the internet, world wide web, current events magazines, among others), provide subject matter for pupil acquisition. These materials may then be used as learning activities by adapting each to the present achievement levels of learners. They may be used as initiating activities, developmental experiences, or culminating experiences in ongoing units of study (Ediger, 2009).

Third, a variety of methods of instruction need to be used in meeting individual needs of learners. To meet these needs, pupils may experience the following:

- problem solving whereby an hypothesis is developed in answer to a question. The hypothesis emphasizes deliberation and is tentative, subject to evaluation and modification.
- project methods in which a unit related construction activity is planned, completed and evaluated.
- textbook methods whereby readiness for its reading is developed through viewing related illustrations, discussing new vocabulary terms and identifying questions. Followup experiences include discussing subject matter read and making use of its content such as dramatizing major ideas read, summarizing, drawing related illustrations, developing a chart, and/or making a model.
- inductive procedures in which pupils achieve generalizations through a learning by discovery procedure.
- deductive approaches in which pupils apply generalizations to a new situation.

- small group methods in which each pupil has opportunities to have input into a discussion in an atmosphere of respect toward others.
- large group sessions whereby pupils are introduced to a new lesson with the use of an AV aid.
- individual methods in which the learner pursues a purposeful activity on his/her own in the social studies.
- an art experience which relates directly to the ongoing lesson presentation.
- research opportunity whereby the pupil pursues and writes up information dealing with a vital topic (Ediger, 2008a).

Providing for each learner is important in order to extend and provide indepth experiences. The needs of the individual must be met so that present and future abilities of pupils have chances of growing, developing, and achieving.

Fourth, pupils need to have decision making responsibilities in school and in society. To make choices, from among alternatives, provides realistic experiences for pupils. Thus, in school and in the societal arenas, the pupil, may be bombarded with choices which need to be made:

- What to do in one's spare time.
- How to proceed in making a model in the social studies.
- Which topic to select to write about in an ongoing lesson.
- How to divide up responsibilities in doing a group project.

Being able to plan well where cooperation is involved may become a part of every person's responsibilities throughout one's lifetime. Being a cordial participant and working together harmoniously with others is salient in making progress in goal attainment. There are social studies teachers who have developed several learning centers in a classroom. Pupils may select which tasks to complete from these centers. Decision making is involved. The choices to be made involve the following, among others:

- completing an individual or committee activity.
- doing an art, a reading/writing, or construction project.
- choosing committee members to work with (Ediger, 2008b).

The above lists a few of the many choices which need to be made in a learning centers approach in the teaching of the social studies. Being involved in small group work is essential presently as well as in future citizenship endeavors.

Fifth, quality sequence in learning makes for more optimal achievement. The social studies teacher must think in terms of ordered learnings for pupils. Thus, what is taught must be related to the immediate past experiences of learners. The present and past experiences of pupils need to be related, not isolated from each other. Thus, pupils may be assisted to develop their own knowledge and skills, known as constructionist psychology. For example in a discussion, pupils may reveal a lack of understanding of the concept "The Crusades." As the discussion continues, the teacher helps pupils to attach understanding to that concept by raising questions pertaining to its meaning. The teacher does not tell its meaning but assists pupils to discover a definition. This is opposite of lecture whereby the teacher would provide its exact contextual definition. Constructivism stresses that the social studies teacher helps pupils to discover knowledge as sequential learnings are found. With lecture, the teacher determines subsequent learnings for pupils each step along the way. Thus with unknown words, the teacher determines how to define each, hoping the learner will understand what is taught. Here, the communication is a one way street in that subject matter moves from the communicator (the teacher) to the communicatee which is the pupil (See Beer, *et al.*, 2008). Sixth, a good current events program needs to be in the offing. Thus, separate sections on the bulletin board should be devoted to news clips and each discussed pertaining to:

- local news such as salient happenings on the local scene.
- happenings and news on the state level including election for state officers.

- news on the national level including campaigns for and election of officials on the national level and budgetary items, among others.
- world happenings including wars, trade among nations, and unemployment data.

Each news item needs thorough discussion and extended to other vital relationships. A democracy depends upon a well informed citizenry (See Keefe, 2007).

Seventh, a quality evaluation program must be in the offing to ascertain learner achievement and progress. The evaluation methods must be valid in that it measures what it purports to measure. Thus if the evaluation items measure problem solving skills, it must do so and not measure something else such as capitol cities of respective nations. Then too, the evaluation methods must emphasize reliability. Thus, consistency of results for a pupils are important in the evaluation dimension, For example, if a pupil ranks on the thirtieth percentile the first time a test is taken and on the eightieth percentile on the same test taken the second time, the question arises, "What is the pupil's test results when they vary much from the thirtieth to the eightieth percentile on the same test?" Reliability is certainly lacking. Upon examination of the print out of pupil test results, the following might be noticed:

- some of the test items lacked clarity in writing due to vagueness in content.
- the vocabulary in test writing was not appropriate for the pupils' stage of development and maturity.
- the test items did not cover what was taught, indicating a lack of validity.
- the test items were not proofed carefully. Omitting a comma, for example, can make for much difference in item interpretation.
- there were too many interpretations of a test item's meaning.
- more than one correct response was possible, but this was not stated in the directions for test taking (See Bracey, 2008).

Recognized standardized tests are pilot tested to take out poorly written test items. The print out from these studies provide the best developers with information on weak test items. These may then be revised. By having test takers take the same test over again, data is secured on test/retest reliability. Most teachers do not do this; perhaps this is due to a lack of time. But, all teachers may use the split/half method to determine reliability. Here, the test is given one time. The odd numbered items are then compared with the even numbered test items. Do those who score highest on the odd numbered items score in a similar manner on the even numbered test items? The computer then may provide a reliability figure in comparing the responses for odd versus even numbered test items. If the test is short in length, the teacher might scan to notice how the two compare with each other. Teachers should become highly knowledgeable about statistics due to information on validity, reliability, percentiles, standard deviations, among others.

On teacher developed tests, the writer has not mentioned anything about ascertaining validity. Here, the test writer may use face validity. Thus, directly after teaching, the teacher writes test items to cover what was taught. Validity, here, emphasizes that what was taught is transfered to one or more multiple choice test items. Then too, the stem and each of the four distractors must be grammatically correct as well as plausible. Plausibility states that there are no ridiculous responses; each is rational and makes sense as a distractor.

Teacher observation might well be a highly useful evaluation technique, providing that quality standards are used here. The social studies teacher may then appraise the following:

- pupil time on task.
- resilience of the learner.
- motivation to achieve.
- harmoniously working together with others.
- curiosity in subject matter as well as in environmental learnings.

- respect for others.

Each of the above provides data for assisting pupils to achieve. Analysis and remediation might then well provide for sequential learning.

In Closing

There are selected trends which social studies teachers need to follow. These trends provide a social studies program for pupils which is of high quality as well as being relevant. The best of objectives, learning opportunities to achieve the objectives, as well as appraisal techniques, must be used as tools to optimize learner achievement and progress in the social studies.

REFERENCES

Beer, *et al.*, (2008), "Summer Learning Camps: Helping Students Prepare for College," *College Student Journal*, 42 (3), 930-938.

Bracey, Gerald B. (2008), "Research, The Algebra Hoax," *Phi Delta Kappa*, 90 (4), 306-307. Mr. Bracey writes highly informative items on research in each issue of the *Phi Delta Kappan*.

Ediger, Marlow (2008a), "Leadership in the School Setting," *Education*, 129(1), 17-20.

Ediger, Marlow (2008b),"The School and Students in Society," *Journal of Instructional Psychology*, 35 (3), 261-263.

Ediger, Marlow (2009), "Scope in the Social Studies," *Edutracks*, 8 (6), 14-16.

Fitzhugh, Will (2006), "Where's the Content?" *Educational Leadership*, 64(2), 42-47.

Keefe, James W. (2007), "What is Personalization?" *Phi Delta Kappan*, 217-224.

Parker, Walter C. (2001). *Social Studies in Elementary Education*. Upper Saddle River, New Jersey: Prentice-Hall, Inc.

39 The Student Teacher and the Social Studies

What kind of experiences in the teaching of the social studies sequence would best equip the future teacher to do well as a professional? The pre-service university curriculum should stress that which assists the student teacher to secure a repertoire of quality experiences in the teaching of the social studies. A highly knowledgeable student teacher of the social sciences, possessing skill in teaching pupils, should aid learners in the public schools to possess subject matter knowledge and social skills to do well in society (Ediger, 2008).

Undergraduate Sequence

The pre-service teacher needs to have a general education background which prepares the individual in becoming proficient as a regular teacher. Too frequently, the pre-service program is separated from teaching and learning situations in the public schools. Rather, it should become integrated. Thus, freshmen English classes need to stress ingredients making for quality writing. Much written work indicative of diverse purposes in writing must be in the offing. For example, in writing an essay, the following need emphasis in actual writing experiences:

- topic sentences at the beginning or end of a paragraph, or inferred.
- sequence of ideas within a paragraph.

- carefully chosen words to clarify meanings (See Bhuvaneswari, 2008, for a discussion on Psycho Linguistic Intervention Strategies).

Coursework in the pre-service English sequence need to be demanding. University students need to be highly proficient in possessing writing skills so that these may be adapted to the developmental level of the pupil as well as modeled later in the student teaching experience. Literature courses need to stress comprehension strategies and analyzing the study of novels in terms of characterization, setting, point of view, satire and plot. Speaking experiences should reflect a clear voice with appropriate stress, pitch, juncture, and enunciation. In written work and in speaking activities, each undergraduate student must demonstrate proficiency and not fall through the cracks due to too many students being in a class. English professors need to be highly competent and take much interest in student achievement and progress. They need to meet periodically with each student to notice if proper standards and criteria are being achieved. The professor serves as a model for teaching and needs to show this model in diverse teaching situations (Ediger and Rao 2007).

Prospective social studies teachers need to have a thorough grounding in the social sciences. Each of the following courses must be demanding and students must show that content is being mastered:

- history with its relevant past in the curriculum, in courses including World History, The Middle East, Latin American and American History, Asiatic as well as European History.
- geography as a separate subject as well as being integrated into the history curriculum.
- economics with emphasis upon recessions, depressions, mortgage meltdowns, goods and services.
- political science with studies of the role of government. on the local, state and national levels, as well as the United Nations.

- anthropology/sociology with stress placed upon how culture affects the human being (See Parker, 2001).

Each of the above social sciences has implications for human behavior and how it influences the individual and group in society. Professors of the social sciences need to have high expectations for each student in possessing needed facts, concepts, and generalizations, useful for the self as a member in society and for teaching. They need to develop within students an understanding of salient knowledge and methods used to acquire content by social scientists.

Pre-service teachers must become proficient in content pertaining to the earth, physical, and biological sciences. They need to achieve excellence in course objectives in each of the above named sciences. Laboratory methods must be carefully supervised and a thorough process of evaluation of learner achievement and progress must be in evidence. Models of teaching quality by professors need to be there for pre-service teachers to emulate (Ediger, 2008).

Mathematics in the general education sequence need to be taught indepth with careful monitoring by professors to assist in optimal student achievement and progress. It, again, is important to monitor carefully those who are planning to become teachers to reveal optimal attainment. Strong student effort and positive attitudes are always salient (See Phillips, *et al.*, 2008).

Undergraduate students need to engage in field experiences, directly related to the teaching of social studies in the public schools. Here, students may observe pupils in the classroom setting, work with small groups and individuals, evaluate the kinds of misunderstandings which pupils possess, and notice general progress made by learners. If the pre-service teacher will be teaching in a self-contained classroom, he/she should be involved in working with pupils in the different subject matter areas. Methods of teaching may and do cut across each academic discipline.

In the professional course sequence, pre-service teachers must experience educational psychology in its diverse manifestations. Undergraduate students should have ample opportunities to see how each of the following psychologies operates in actual teaching and learning situations:

- use of behaviorism and measurable stated objectives.
- implementation of problem solving and project methods.
- emphasis upon pupil choices and decision making in the curriculum as in learning centers.
- holism in the instructional arena (See Thyagu, *et al.*, 2009).

A thorough grounding in the philosophy of education which stresses the following is also salient for prospective to teachers to not only study these schools of thought, but also see them operationalized:

- realism with emphasis placed upon measurably stated objectives in teaching.
- existentialism stressing the human condition, as in literature.
- idealism emphasizing the "categorical imperative" as viewed by Immanuel Kant.
- experimentalism which integrates ideas in teaching pertaining to school and society (See John Dewey, 1916).

Educational psychology and philosophy courses become meaningful and challenging when practical applications are made of each in the public school classroom.

Measurement and evaluation course work needs to be meaningful and useful to pre-service teachers. Indepth learning and demonstrated accomplishment must be in the offing for the following, among others:

- writing and critiquing teacher written tests.
- devising valid and reliable testing instruments to appraise pupil achievement in the social studies.
- understanding the concepts of percentiles, standard deviation, the normal distribution curve, as well as quartile deviation.

- attaching meaning to research studies involving experimental studies, correlations and descriptive studies.
- examining and appraising norm and criterion referenced tests.
- evaluating the concepts *formative* and *summative* tests, as well as *benchmarks* of instruction (See Ormrod, 2007).

Methods of teaching the social studies are highly significant and should be integrated with field experiences and seminars. Thus, pre-service teachers are assisted in applying what was learned in the university classroom. Methods of teaching the social studies should emphasize the following:

- unit construction based on sound research, educational psychology and philosophical thought.
- mini-lessons taught and appraised in the classroom setting.
- field studies in which social studies methods are tried out in the public school classroom.
- conferences held with the university supervisor pertaining to field work experiences in the social studies
- tests given to students to indicate achievement and progress in methods courses. Diagnosis and remediation is involved here (See Reilly, 2007).

Faculty teaching social studies methods courses need to present a model to prospective teachers who will be working with pupils in the public schools.

Student teaching is the capstone or final experience of the undergraduate sequence in education. Here, the student teacher needs to integrate and relate previous university experiences leading to:

- the pre-service teacher taking part in all responsibilities subsequently of a full time regular teacher.
- observing and participating in the classroom under the guidance of a quality cooperating teacher.
- managing a classroom of learners, grouping for instruction and observing pupil achievement and progress.

- engaging pupils in meaningful learning.
- developing and designing units of study and daily lesson plans.
- assisting pupils in small groups and individual study.
- teaching in large group sessions.
- pupils self-evaluation and responsible behavior.
- interacting positively with the school administrator and with other classroom teachers (See National Council for the Social Studies, 2008).

The student teacher needs to be appraised frequently by the supervisor in order to improve instruction. Also, it is good to conduct a seminar with other student teachers supervised by the supervisor. The seminar needs to include:

- discussions on problems faced in student teaching and possible remedial actions taken.
- suggestions for improving teaching and learning situations.
- the use of teaching materials/experiences such as AV aids, DVDs, electronic readers, the internet, the world wide web, basal textbooks, excursions, among others.
- making of teaching aids to assist in the instructional arena.

Innovative methods of teaching to observe by the student teacher include:

- team teaching and flexible grouping.
- cooperative learning, as well as peer teaching and learning.
- problem solving, project methods, as well as critical and creative thinking situations.
- the integrated social studies curriculum.
- use of primary sources in teaching history (See Pace. 2007).

Each of the above named plans need to be analyzed for discussion purposes. University students need to see the pros and cons of each plan.

In closing

It cannot be emphasized too much that high quality is essential in these endeavors. Social studies teachers need to assist in developing knowledgeable good citizens who can function well in school and in society.

REFERENCES

Bhuvaneswari, S. (2008), Effect of Psycho Linguistic Intervention Strategies in Enhancing Writing Competency in English Among High school Learners. Alagappa University, Karaikudi, India. Ph D thesis appraised by Marlow Ediger.

Dewey, John (1916), *Democracy and Education*. New York: The Macmillan Company.

Ediger, Marlow (2008), "Leadership in the School Setting," *Education*, 129 (1), 17-20.

Ediger, Marlow and Digumarti Bhaskara Rao (2007), *Language Arts Education*. New Delhi, India: Discovery Publishing House (Ltd.).

Ediger, Marlow (2008), "The Old Order Amish and the Social Studies," Viewpoints, 38 (4), 14-16.

National Council for the Social Studies (2008), "A Vision of Powerful Teaching and Learning in the Social Studies," *Social Education*, 72 (5), 277-280.

Ormrod, Jeanne Ellis (2007), *Educational Psychology*, Sixth Edition, Chapter Twelve.

Pace, Judith L. (December 18, 2007), "Why We Need To Save (and Strengthen), Social Studies," Education Week.

Parker, Walter C. (2001), *Social Studies in Elementary Education*. Upper Saddle River, New Jersey: Charles E. Merrill.

Phillips, *et al.* (2008), "Enhancing a Curriculum: A Focus on the Developmental Process," *College Student Journal*, 42(4), 1070-1074.

Reilly, Mary Ann (2007), "Choice of Action: Using Data to Make Instructional decisions in Kindergarten," *The Reading Teacher*, 60 (8), 770-775.

Thyagu, *et al.*, (2009), "Mobile Learning is Future Learning," *Edutracks*, 8 (6), 5-8.

Problems in School Curriculum Development

There are selected problems in curriculum development which need to be resolved. These problems relate to pupil learning in ongoing units of study and involve what is relevant and salient to learn. Determining revisions and modifications in curriculum development need to be continuous and ongoing. As pupils and society change, so must the school curriculum. The curriculum of the past is no longer useful presently. Thus, which changes and modifications need to be made in the curriculum?

Curriculum Trends

A major change which must be made pertains to what is *significant* for pupil learning. With emphasis having been placed upon mandated objectives of instruction, teachers have been pressured to teach what will be tested. Reading and mathematics then have received primary attention. High stakes testing stresses that each pupil pass a mandated test to be promoted to the next higher grade level. This leaves out selected curriculum areas. Science has just recently been added to the mandated areas for testing, but it still leaves out others which are highly important (Ediger, 2008).

Test results should compare a pupil's present achievement with his/her past measurable achievement to notice progress. This is salient for parents to notice achievement of a son/daughter from one time to the next. Also, diagnostic results must indicate what teachers and parents need to provide assistance in, so that sequential progress may be in the offing for the pupil (Ediger, 2008).

The most important objectives for pupil attainment may not be emphasized in the curriculum. These include the following:

- caring for the welfare of others, especially those who have disabilities.
- assisting others in need; this also stresses helping pupils academically as the need arises.
- working cooperatively with others in a project related to an ongoing unit of study.
- wanting to do quality work in school and in society.
- being a good citizen by helping to improve the human condition in society (See Sapon-Shevin, 2008).

The asterisked items listed above are difficult to emphasize in teaching and learning situations as well as being difficult to ascertain and measure pupil achievement and progress therein. To begin with, the teacher may serve as a model in caring, assisting and working cooperatively. He/she should call attention in class of pupils showing specific acts involving these behaviors. As much as possible, these kinds of objectives need to be stressed in ongoing lifelike situations. Merely memorizing traits of good behavior is not adequate! A doing approach is much superior.

Attitudinal Objectives

There are salient objectives which need to be emphasized, but are not in the realm of mandated tested nor can they be classified as subject matter. These come under the *attitudes* heading. For example, "empathy" is such a concept which may be stated as an objective for pupil attainment. Thus, learning of academic content, by itself, is to be prized, but it leaves out how an individual relates to others. Empathy stresses:

- possessing positive feelings towards others.

- having consideration for people and their accomplishments.
- being able to 'step into the shoes' of others and understand their feelings.
- understanding how negative teasing hurts others.
- frowning upon rudeness, harassment, gossip and intimidation.

Pupil achievement is hindered when negative statements are made to and about others. For example, pupils may fear coming to school when harassment is in evidence, or learners become timid when intimidation is present. The writer when supervising university student teachers in the public schools noticed numerous cases of harassment such as a pupil:

- kicking another child under the classroom desk after sharpening his pencil.
- hitting another learner after returning to his seat from asking a question of the teacher.
- ridiculing an answer given by a pupil.
- being extremely rude with remarks made to a child when going out to recess.
- rubbing a pupil's ears, when no one was watching, until they were red, while waiting for the school bus (See Crawford, 2008).

Our fifth grade son cried at home one evening when his mother noticed black spots on his ankles. He finally said what had happened. A bully on the school bus would kick his ankles if he did not pay money to avoid the terror. Our son feared grave repercussions if his mother and I would tell the bus driver or the director of school transportation of these happenings. We went to the director of school transportation in this city of 18,000 people and told him what had happened and our son's repercussion fears. The director was very empathetic and said this would not happen again and to not fear any consequences. It worked! There was no more terror money paid to the perpetrator of the kicking and he behaved perfectly on the school bus the rest of the school year. It is extremely difficult for parents to know what to do in these cases. If it had not worked, we had an alternative plan in mind to resolve the conflict. The director of school transportation, or other authorized person, must act quickly; there is no time for continuous bruising to occur.

Rules to curtail harassing need to be clear and must be communicated to pupils, teachers and school administrators. There need to be immediate penalties and punishments due the transgressor. These need to be spelled out with clarity. To harass is not good for the harasser; it builds a negative self image. To receive any kind of 'reward' for harassing hinders in achieving good will and a positive self image. Harassing can only bring on bad consequences as this act continues. Who knows what the receiver of the harassment will do to the perpetrator? It is best, of course, to avoid any of these happenings to occur.

A third problem in curriculum development pertains to the need for cooperation. Too frequently, competition has been the rule of the day when the only good is for a child to outdo the other. Thus, it is imperative that pupils learn to work together for the common good of all in a classroom. Extreme cases of competition may result in:

- cheating to get ahead of others in academic classroom tests, copying a report as one's own on a selected topic from a computer printout, and giving excuses (lying) for assignments not completed.
- paying others to do one's class assignments.
- threatening others to not "work as hard" thus lowering class standards for the former to get ahead.
- tripping others on the playground and in class. There are numerous cases whereby a pupil sticks his/her leg out to trip others who go to the teacher's desk for assistance or to sharpen a pencil. Feelings of embarrassment hinder pupil achievement and progress. So often, too, feelings of revenge come about in these situations (See Merwin, 2005).

Classroom rules need to be established which stress quality work habits and these must become a part of the repertoire of the pupil. A major rule should be that pupils do not say or do anything mean to others. Examples of this rule and other rules need to be given so that each truly understands mean behavior which includes harassment. It must be discussed meaningfully how negative behavior hinders others from achieving as optimally as possible. Humiliation does not make for positive feelings or for friendship making (Ediger, 2007).

Subject Matter Learnings

Academic content needs to be relevant and possesses practical usage. Learning content for the sake of doing so will not be too encouraging to most learners. In the study of history, pupils need to draw conclusions as to what can be used presently from learnings of the past. For example, in studying units on world history, the fighting of wars not only bankrupted nations but also caused tremendous damage to moral judgments. Deaths in combat, loss of limbs, brain damage, and mental illness, resulted from wars along with property/land damage. Incorporated skills include problem solving, critical and creative thinking (See Dash, 2008).

Project methods may be stressed in ongoing units of study such as pupils with teacher guidance:

- developing a model village in a region prior to and after involved armed forces inflicted damages.
- an agricultural area showing luscious farm crops followed by sequential illustrations showing their destruction, as a result of war.
- doing a model refugee camp for those having lost homes from armed conflict.

There are a plethora of possibilities when pupil/teacher planning is involved. Ample input from the learner is necessary based on background knowledge possessed. The following are considerations for pupil/teacher planning:

- interests involved in doing a specific project.
- maturity level of the learner.
- meaningful learning being accrued in that the project must make sense as well as possess purpose.

- the learning style of the pupil in preferring individual versus committee endeavors (See Ness, 2007).

The planned and completed project may be shown within the classroom with other classes being invited to view the displays. Questions may then be asked by viewers. These questions might well provide fodder for more indepth studies. Personal initiative is salient in doing projects.

In closing

Curriculum development involves much planning in terms of objectives for pupils to attain, learning opportunities to achieve the objectives and evaluation procedures to ascertain achievement and progress. There are diverse kinds of activities for learner engagement to achieve, develop and grow. This includes technology use. Regardless of the mode of instruction, pupils must understand what is taught, be fully engaged in learning, perceive value in achieving, and be able to apply facts, concepts and generalizations acquired.

REFERENCES

Crawford, Marilyn (2008), "Thinking Inside the Clock," *Phi Delta Kappan*, 90(4), 251-255.

Dash, Neena (2008), "Decision-Making in Schools," *Edutracks*, 8(4), 10-12.

Ediger, Marlow (2007), "Preparing School Administrators," *Reading Improvement*, 44 (3), 149-152.

Ediger, Marlow (2008), "The School and Students in Society," *Journal of Instructional Psychology*, 35 (3), 260-263.

Ediger, Marlow (2008), "Leadership in the School Setting," *Education*, 129(1), 17-20.

Merwin, Michelle Marks (2005), "On Being Respected or Liked: Principle Centered Teaching," *College Student Journal*, 39 (4), 798-805.

Ness, Molly (2007), "Reading Comprehension Strategies in Secondary Content-Area Classrooms," *Phi Delta Kappan*, 89 (3), 229-231.

Sapon-Shevin, Mara (2008), "Learning in an Inclusive Community," *Educational Leadership*, 66 (1), 49-53.

Spelling in School Curriculum

The spelling curriculum has truly undergone a plethora of changes during the decades. Incorporated for each day of the week, during 1930s and 1940s in USA, were the following examples:

- **Monday:** Introduction of new weekly words by the teacher with pupils following along in the basal text as each new word is pronounced with the teacher defining new words. Pupils would correctly pronounce each word after the teacher had done so. Each word in the weekly list was written in practice ten times.
- **Tuesday:** Pupils briefly reviewed the correct spelling of each word from the list and then took a written test as the teacher pronounced each word. After the spelled words were checked for correctness by the teacher, pupils individually were to spell correctly those words which were misspelled. Each misspelled word was written correctly.
- **Wednesday:** The teacher pointed out why selected words were misspelled on Tuesday by viewing handwriting and phonic elements. Thus, the following, among others, contained problems in spelling due to inconsistency between symbol and sound: phone ("ph" letters making the "f" sound; the letter "d" reversed in manuscript writing with "b." A game was played whereby there were two sides in the classroom. The teacher pronounced a word from the current spelling

list and the pupil, at the chalkboard, who was first in correct spelling would receive a point for his/her side. Then the next two pupils, one from each side, would go to the blackboard; the teacher would pronounce a different word orally. The child who spelled the word correctly received a point for his/her side. This activity, in sequence, lasted approximately 20 minutes, according to the daily schedule.

- **Thursday:** Pupils reviewed their weekly spelling words and then took a trial test. Those who scored 100 per cent correct need not take the final test on Friday.
- **Friday:** The remainder of the pupils took the final test on all the listed words from the weekly spelling list.

Modifications and Revisions

The spelling plan for each weekly list of word to be mastered was not all bad. Many learned to spell words well and seemingly communicated highly effectively in written work, over the years, including my doctoral dissertation. Now, many learned to use the word processor and use standardized approaches in utilizing the key board, not the hunt and peck system. When reading Journal articles, many feel that educators, today, believe everything written in the past was quackery in eduction. Not so. We would like to review the above-named plan for learning to spell words which we experienced and make suggested modifications. Each idea presented needs to be taken flexibly and adapted to pupils in a specific classroom. On Monday and Tuesday, for example, we would have pupils carefully view the spelling words, as each word is pointed to in large, neatly printed words in manuscript on the white/chalk board. Involve children in correctly pronouncing the spelling words and in as many activities as possible. A lack of consistency between symbol and sound, as swell as selected consistencies may be pointed out. Learners need to be guided in using these words in sentences. The teacher needs to model several methodologies in learning to spell words. The following are selected ways, among others:

- writing each word five times as chosen by the learner.
- using each spelling word in an oral/written sentence.
- writing a single paragraph containing as many new words as possible.
- doing a poem, rhymed or unrhymed, incorporating new spelling words.
- miming selected spelling words and having classmates guess what is being mimed.
- performing a reader's theater, incorporating ensuing spelling words.

Pupils individually should ascertain their best way of learning to spell words. Concrete results from pupils are utilized to appraise methods used by pupils in mastering these words from functional as well as from tests on the weekly list. The number of words per week to be mastered may well depend upon how much motivation is developed and present achievement levels of individual learners. Too frequently, pupils may do well on weekly tests, but fail to spell the same words correctly in written work in ongoing units of study (Ediger and Rao, 2011).

As much as possible, the teacher needs to challenge pupils to make use of each spelling word studied. Wednesday, pupils may work on the following activities containing the new spelling words:

- doing/developing crossword puzzles.
- evaluating paragraphs with misspelled words and making necessary corrections.
- keeping a journal/diary on daily or weekly experiences in spelling.
- writing invitations, announcements, and simple plays which incorporate the new words in spelling.
- maintaining a traditional/electronic portfolio on revealing progress made in spelling.
- utilizing technology in written work such as the word processor and spell check.

In Closing

Technology will continue to weaken the need for tradition, as it should, in order to improve products and processes in the communication arenas. However, there will be purposes in learning to spell words correctly within the framework of writing for the following reasons:

- to use spell check, the writers has to be reasonably close to spelling correctly an incorrect word; otherwise the monitor might not come up with possible correct spellings.
- a word processor will not always be available for writing.
- texting messages is very informal with highly abbreviated spellings and is very limited in written work within more formal, approved settings including college/university course work, as well as demands at a workplace.
- it may be handier to write in manuscript/cursive writing, in selected writing situations, such as making a shopping list, writing notes as reminders, among others.

Pupils need to become good writers which is useful in school and at the workplace. Evafuators, in hiring positions, may well look at the quality and ability of individuals to communicate effectively in writing. Purpose, interests, needs, utility, and meaning are quality indicators in determining the spelling/writing curriculum.

REFERENCE

Ediger, Marlow, and D. Bhaskara Rao (2011), *Essays on Teaching Reading*. New Delhi, India: Discovery Publishing House (Ltd.).

Seven Criteria for an Effective Classroom Environment for an Effective Curriculum Transaction

There are a plethora of variables which affect pupils in the classroom. These might involve the obvious such as uncomfortable temperature readings a well as the following:

* small group work as compared to individual activities.
* use of measurably stated objectives versus constructivism as psychologies of learning.
* a very quiet environment compared to business like surroundings.
* zero tolerance in discipline as compared to pupil/teacher planning of rules for classroom conduct.
* teacher directed learning activities compared to a learner centered approach.
* lecture/explanations versus critical and creative thinking as well as problem solving experiences.
* traditional seating arrangements in rows and columns as compared to flexible room arrangements (Ediger and Rao, 2005).

In each of the above-asterisked items, committees need to work on solutions to these issues in order to resolve the dilemmas. Committees individually need to report to the total group to seek input. Eventually, several approaches may be used such as individual as well as group endeavors to meet needs of learners. Teachers and school administrators benefit when diverse ideas are presented and research is done to gather necessary information in formulating conclusions, following much deliberation. Beyond these items listed above, an appropriate related classroom environment must be in the offing in teaching and learning situations. This environment facilitates pupils achievement of relevant objectives of instruction.

Favorable Learning Environments

Proactive strategies need to be in the offing to minimize/ eliminate negative behavior such as harassing others. Being harassed hinders pupil achievement and progress. Relevant rules discussed with pupils and adequate supervision should assist in identifying cases of harassment. These cases need to be handled in a way in which pupils can perceive the harm inflicted on others when harassment is in evidence. Not only does the victim feel hurt, but the perpetrator tries to get away with what he/she feels is manly or womanly. But, in all reality, it is humiliating to both. Inwardly, the perpetrator sees the consequences of his/her acts. No one likes to be called unwanted names, be mimicked with unbecoming language, being hurt physically and or experience emotional damage. Pupils experiencing harassment should have a place to report grievances. A counselor, well versed in this area, should respond immediately to cases of harassment. The victim needs to be listened to carefully and the perpetrator needs imme-diate counseling to modify and change behavior (See Ahmad, 2009).

Second, classroom rules need to assist in avoiding misbehavior of pupils. Misbehavior might well consist of bothering others to hinder learning, including bursts of anger and talking back to the teacher. Politeness toward others, involving both teachers and learners, is essential for any classroom to perform and function well. A community of learners emphasizes cooperation in developing an environment conducive to optimal pupil achievement in academic, social, and psychomotor skills (Ediger, 2009).

Third, pupils from different cultural groups must be accepted as individuals having much worth. No one desires to be excluded, but wishes to possess feelings of belonging. Recent immigrants from abroad should not be shunned, but rather integrated so they can reveal talents possessed through their native art, dress, music, language, dances, as well as foods eaten. Sharing of culture broadens educational horizons of classmates and enriches lives. There are diverse ways of meeting personal needs and human culture reveals these differences (See Sapon-Shevin, 2008). For example when eating with bedouins in the Middle East, the writer observed smacking of lips is good in order to show excellence in tasty foods eaten, but in the US, of course, it violates folkways and morays.

Fourth, pupils need to have ample opportunities to work in cooperative learning situations. They need rules to follow such as each pupil in the committee being actively involved, ideas circulating among members in the group, politeness and consideration for others being stressed, and clarity of content being expressed by pupils. Classroom environments improve when criteria are used to foster positive human relationships. Each participant in learning must be valued and quality human values must pervade instruction (See Petress, 2006).

Fifth, pupils individually need to feel important for personal accomplishments be it in school or in society. For example, if a slow learner improves in achieving, this needs to be rewarded with praise for actual accomplishments. There are numerous rewards given pupils for achieving outside the school setting, such as 4H, Boys and Girl Scouts, Boys and Girls' Clubs and FFA, among others, which provide opportunities for pupil recognition in the school setting. Esteem needs must be met of learners. These assist pupils to develop motivational feelings to realize higher levels of attainment. The classroom teacher must assist pupils to feel motivation to reach out, grow and accomplish. Talents of learners individually need to be adequately provided for in the school setting. Receiving recognition for attained goals is significant for anyone in the classroom, teachers included. There is certainly nothing wrong with a teacher saying what he/she accomplished in school and in society. Teacher achievement is a model for others to emulate (Ediger, 2008).

Sixth, the feeling dimension is too frequently omitted in teaching and learning situations. Perhaps, much of this is due to the testing movement whereby scores on mandated tests receive the most attention in a school day. These tests focus on academic achievement. Cognitive objectives are then emphasized highly and attitudinal (affective) ends receive short schrift. Advocates of Emotional IQs stress the importance of the feeling dimension in school and at the work place. Thus, a person may have high subject matter knowledge, but get along very poorly with others. Individuals are dismissed from various jobs because of having poor attitudes toward work, the work place, and toward those employed there. Rude, inconsiderate behaviors are the downfall of these individuals. Learning activities which are satisfying and perceived worthwhile helps pupils to develop well emotionally (See Booker, 2008).

Seventh, pupils must understand what is taught and not merely memorize subject matter for a test. Meaning attached to ongoing experiences helps learners to achieve sequentially. Subsequent activities are built upon previously acquired knowledge and skills. The ensuing then becomes comprehensible and readiness for learning is then in evidence. Interests, too, are fostered if meaning is there.

REFERENCES

Ahmad, Saijad (2009), "Evolving a Framework for Teaching and Learning," *Edutracks*, 8 (9), 11-12.

Booker, Keonya (2008), "The Role of Instructors and Peers in Establishing a Classsroom Community," Journal of Instructional *Psychology*, 35 (1), 12-16.

Ediger, Marlow (2009), "Technical Education, the Work Place, and the Student," *American Technical Education Journal* (ATEA), 36 (2), 18-19.

Ediger, Marlow (2008), "Current Events in the Social Studies," *Social Studies Review*, 47 (2), 58-60.

Ediger, Marlow and Digumarti Bhaskara Rao (2005), *Quality School Education*. New Delhi, India: Discovery Publishing House (Ltd.).

Petress, Ken (2006), "An Operational Definition of Class Participation," *College Student Journal*, 40 (4), 821-823.

Sapon-Shevin, Mara (2008), "Learning in an Inclusive Classroom," *Educational Leadership*, 66 (1), 49-53.

43 The School

A school is an institution designed for the teaching of students (or "pupils") under the direction of teachers. Most countries have systems of formal education, which is commonly compulsory. In these systems, students progress through a series of schools. The names for these schools vary by country but generally include primary school for young children and secondary school for teenagers who have completed primary education. An institution where higher education is taught, is commonly called a university college or university.

In addition to these core schools, students in a given country may also attend schools before and after primary and secondary education. Kindergarten or pre-school provide some schooling to very young children (typically ages 3-5). University, vocational school, college or seminary may be available after secondary school. A school may also be dedicated to one particular field, such as a school of economics or a school of dance. Alternative schools may provide non-traditional curriculum and methods.

There are also non-government schools, called private schools. Private schools may be required when the government does not supply adequate, or special education. Other private schools can also be religious, such as Christian schools, hawzas, yeshivas, and others; or schools that have a higher standard of education or seek to foster other personal achievements. Schools for adults include institutions of corporate training, Military education and training and business schools.

In home-schooling and online schools, teaching and learning take place outside of a traditional school building.

Etymology

The word *school* derives from Greek αχολ'η *(scholē)*, originally meaning "leisure" and also "that in which leisure is employed", but later "a group to whom lectures were given, school".

History and Development of Schools

The concept of grouping students together in a centralized location for learning has existed since Classical antiquity. Formal schools have existed at least since ancient Greece, ancient Rome, ancient India, and ancient China. The Byzantine Empire had an established schooling system beginning at the primary level. According to *Traditions and Encounters,* the founding of the primary education system began in AD 425 and "... military personnel usually had at least a primary education ...". The sometimes efficient and often large government of the Empire meant that educated citizens were a must. Although Byzantium lost much of the grandeur of Roman culture and extravagance in the process of surviving, the Empire emphasized efficiency in its war manuals. The Byzantine education system continued until the empire's collapse in AD 1453.

Islam was another culture that developed a school system in the modem sense of the word. Emphasis was put on knowledge, which required a systematic way of teaching and spreading knowledge, and purpose-built structures. At first, mosques combined both religious performance and learning activities, but by the 9th century, the Madrassa was introduced, a proper school that was built independently from the mosque. They were also the first to make the *Madrassa* system a public domain under the control of the Caliph. The Nizamiyya madrasa is considered by consensus of scholars to be the earliest surviving school, built towards AD 1066 by Emir Nizam Al-Mulk.

Under the Ottomans, the towns of Bursa and Edirne became the main centers of learning. The Ottoman system of Külliye, a building complex containing a mosque, a hospital, madrassa, and public kitchen and dining areas, revolutionized the education system, making learning accessible to a wider public through its free meals, health care and sometimes free accommodation.

The 19th century historian, Scott holds that a remarkable correspondence exists between the procedure established by those institutions and the methods of the present day. They had their collegiate courses, their prizes for proficiency in scholarship, their oratorical and poetical contests, their commencements and their degrees. In the department of medicine, a severe and prolonged examination, conducted by the most eminent physicians of the capital, was exacted of all candidates desirous of practicing their profession, and such as were unable to stand the test were formally pronounced incompetent.

In Europe during the Middle Ages and much of the Early Modern period, the main purpose of schools (as opposed to universities) was to teach the Latin language. This led to the term grammar school, which in the United States informally refers to a primary school, but in the United Kingdom means a school that selects entrants based on ability or aptitude. Following this, the school curriculum has gradually broadened to include literacy in the vernacular language as well as technical, artistic, scientific and practical subjects.

Many of the earlier public schools in the United States were one-room schools where a single teacher taught seven grades of boys and girls in the same classroom. Beginning in the 1920s, one-room schools were consolidated into multiple classroom facilities with transportation increasingly provided by kid hacks and school buses.

Regional Terms

The use of the term *school* varies by country, as do the names of the various levels of education within the country.

United Kingdom and Commonwealth of Nations

In the United Kingdom, the term *school* refers primarily to pre-university institutions and these can, for the most part, be divided into pre-schools or nursery schools, primary schools (sometimes further divided into infant school and junior school), and secondary schools. Various types of secondary schools in England and Wales include grammar schools, comprehensives, secondary moderns, and city academies. In Scotland, while they may have different names, all Secondary schools are the same, except in that they may be funded by the state, or independently funded. It is unclear if "Academies", which are a hybrid between state and independently funded/controlled schools and have been introduced to England in recent years, will ever be introduced to Scotland. School performance in Scotland is monitored by Her Majesty's Inspectorate of Education. Ofsted reports on performance in England and Estyn reports on performance in Wales.

In the United Kingdom, most schools are publicly funded and known as state schools or maintained schools in which tuition is provided free. There are also private schools or independent schools that charge fees. Some of the most selective and expensive private schools are known as public schools, a usage that can be confusing to speakers of North American English. In North American usage, a public school is one that is publicly funded or run.

In much of the Commonwealth of Nations, including Australia, New Zealand, India, Pakistan, Bangladesh, Sri Lanka, South Africa, Kenya and Tanzania, the term *school* refers primarily to pre-university institutions.

India

In ancient India, schools were in the form of *Gurukuls*. *Gurukuls* were traditional Hindu residential schools of learning; typically the teacher's house or a monastery. During the Mughal rule, *Madrasahs* were introduced in India to educate the children of Muslim parents. British records show that indigenous education was widespread in the 18th century, with a school for every temple, mosque or village in most regions of the country. The subjects taught included Reading, Writing, Arithmetic, Theology, Law, Astronomy, Metaphysics, Ethics, Medical Science and Religion.

Under the British rule in India, Christian missionaries from England, USA and other countries established missionary and boarding schools throughout the country. Later as these schools gained in popularity, more were started and some gained prestige. These schools marked the beginning of modern schooling in India and the syllabus and calendar they followed became the benchmark for schools in modern India. Today most of the schools follow the missionary school model in terms of tutoring, subject/syllabus, governance etc.with minor changes. Schools in India range from schools with large campuses with thousands of students and hefty fees to schools where children are taught under a tree with a small/no campus and are totally free of cost. There are various boards of schools in India, namely Central Board for Secondary Education (CBSE), Council for the Indian School Certificate Examinations (CISCE), Madrasa Boards of various states, Matriculation Boards of various states, State Boards of various boards, Anglo Indian Board, and so on. The typical syllabus today includes Language(s), Mathematics, Science - Physics, Chemistry, Biology, Geography, History, General Knowledge, Information Technology/Computer Science etc. Extra curricular activities include physical education/sports and cultural activities like music, choreography, painting, theater/drama etc.

Europe

In much of continental Europe, the term *school* usually applies to primary education, with primary schools that last between four and nine years, depending on the country. It also applies to secondary education, with secondary schools often divided between *Gymnasiums* and vocational schools, which again depending on country and type of school educate students for between three and six years. In Germany students graduating from *Grundschule* are not allowed to directly progress into a vocational school, but are supposed to proceed to one of Germany's general education schools such as Gesamtschule, Hauptschule, Realschule or Gymnasium. When they leave that school, which usually happens at age 15-19 they are allowed to proceed to a vocational school. The term school is rarely used for tertiary education, except for some *upper* or *high* schools (German: Hochschule), which describe colleges and universities.

In Eastern Europe modern schools (after World War II), of both primary and secondary educations, often are combined, while secondary education might be split into accomplished or not. The schools are classified as middle schools of general education and for the technical purposes include "degrees" of the education they provide out of three available: the first - primary, the second - unaccomplished secondary and the third - accomplished secondary. Usually the first two degrees of education (eight years) are always included, while the last one (two years) gives option for the students to pursue vocational or specialized educations.

North America and the United States

In North America, the term *school* can refer to any educational institution at any level and covers all of the following: preschool (for toddlers), kindergarten, elementary school, middle school (also called intermediate school or junior high school, depending on specific age groups and geographic region), senior high school, college, university and graduate school.

In the US, school performance through high school is monitored by each state's Department of Education. Charter schools are publicly funded elementary or secondary schools that have been freed from some of the rules, regulations and statutes that apply to other public schools. The terms grammar school and *grade school* are sometimes used to refer to a primary school.

School Ownership and Operation

Many schools are owned or funded by states. Private schools operate independently from the government. Private schools usually rely on fees from families whose children attend the school for funding; however, sometimes such schools also receive government support (for example, through School vouchers). Many private schools are affiliated with a particular religion; these are known as parochial schools.

Components of most Schools

Schools are organized spaces purposed for teaching and learning. The classrooms, where teachers teach and students learn, are of central importance, but typical schools have many other areas, which may include:

- *Cafeteria* (Commons), dining hall or canteen where students eat lunch and often breakfast and snacks.
- *Athletic field*, playground, gym, and/or track place where students participating in sports or physical education practice.
- *Auditorium or hall* where student theatrical and musical productions can be staged and where all-school events such as assemblies are held.
- *Office* where the administrative work of the school is done.
- *Library* where students consult and check out books and magazines and often use computers.
- *Specialized classrooms* including laboratories for science education.
- *Computer labs* where computer-based work is done and the internet accessed.

School Security

The safety of staff and students is increasingly becoming an issue for school communities, an issue most schools are addressing through improved security. After mass shootings such as the Columbine High School massacre and the Virginia Tech incident, many school administrators in the United States have created plans to protect students and staff in the event of a school shooting. Some have also taken measures such as installing metal detectors or video surveillance. Others have even taken measures such as having the children swipe identification cards as they board the school bus. For some schools, these plans have included the use of door numbering to aid public safety response.

Other security concerns faced by schools include bomb threats, gangs, vandalism and bullying.

School Health Services

School health services are services from medical, teaching and other professionals applied in or out of school to improve the health and well-being of children and in some cases whole families. These services have been developed in different ways around the globe but the fundamentals are constant: the early detection, correction, prevention or amelioration of disease, disability and abuse from which school aged children can suffer.

Online Schools and Classes

Some schools offer remote access to their classes over the Internet. Online schools also can provide support to traditional schools, as in the case of the School Net Namibia. Some online classes provide experience in a class so that when you take it you have already been introduced to the subject and know what to expect and even more classes provide High School/ College credit allowing you to take the class at your own pace. Many online classes cost money to use but some are offered free.

Stress

As a profession, teaching has levels of Work-Related Stress (WRS) that are among the highest of any profession in some countries, such as the United Kingdom. The degree of this problem is becoming increasingly recognized and support systems are being put into place. Teacher education increasingly recognizes the need to train those new to the profession to be aware of and overcome mental health challenges they may face.

Stress sometimes affects students more severely than teachers, up to the point where the students are prescribed stress medication. This stress is claimed to be related to standardized testing and the pressure on students to score above average.

Discipline

Schools and their teachers have always been under pressure—for instance, pressure to cover the curriculum, to perform well in comparison to other schools and to avoid the stigma of being "soft" or "spoiling" toward students. Forms of discipline, such as control over when students may speak, and normalized behaviour, such as raising a hand to speak, are imposed in the name of greater efficiency. Practitioners of critical pedagogy maintain that such disciplinary measures have no positive effect on student learning. Indeed, some argue that disciplinary practices detract from learning, saying that they undermine students' individual dignity and sense of self-worth—the latter occupying a more primary role in students' hierarchy of needs.

REFERENCES

Bentley, Jerry H. (2006). *Traditions & Encounters a Global Perspective on the Past.* New York: McGraw-Hill, p. 331.

"Bulling, Anti-bullying Legislation, and School Safety". School security.org. Retrieved 2009-10-03.

"Children & School Anxiety, Stress Management". Webmd.com. Retrieved 2010-03-28.

Online Etymology Dictionary; H.G. Liddell & R. Scott, A Greek-English Lexicon.

School, on *Oxford Dictionaries.*

"School Vandalism Takes Its Toll". Wrensolutions.com. Retrieved 2009-10-03.

σχολη, Henry George Liddell, Robert Scott, *A Greek-English Lexicon,* on Perseus.

"Survey confirms student stress, but next step is unclear (May 06, 2005)". Paloaltoonline.com. 2005-05-06. Retrieved 2009-10-03.

"Teacher Support for England & Wales". Teachersupport.info. Retrieved 2009-10-03.

"Teacher Support for Scotland". Teachersupport.info. Retrieved 2009-10-03.

"Work-Related Stress in Teaching". Wrsrecovery.com. Retrieved 2009-10-03.

Further Reading

Dodge, B. (1962). *'Muslim Education in the Medieval Times'*, The Middle East Institute, Washington D.C.

Education as Enforcement: The Militarization and Corporatization of Schools, edited by Kenneth J. Saltman and David A. Gabbard, Routledge Falmer 2003.review.

Makdisi, G. (1980). *'On the Origin and Development of the College in Islam and the West'*, in Islam and the Medieval West, ed. Khalil I. Semaan, State University of New York Press.

Nakosteen, M. (1964). *'History of Islamic Origins of Western Education AD 800-1350'*, University of Colorado Press, Boulder, Colorado.

Ribera, J. (1928). *Disertaciones Y Opusculos,* 2 vols. Madrid.

Spielhofer, Thomas, Tom Benton, Sandie Schagen. "A study of the effects of school size and single-sex education in English schools." *Research Papers in Education* June 2004:133159,27.

Toppo, Greg. "High-tech School Security is on the Rise." *USA Today* 9 October 2006.

Traditions and Encounters, by Jerry H. Bentley and Herb F. Ziegler.

Source & Courtesy: *Wikipedia, the free encyclopedia.* Retrieved on 1st November, 2012.

Index

K

L

M

N